Shawn Madigan

Liturgical Spirituality and the Rite of Christian Initiation of Adults

LTP

Liturgy Training Publications
in cooperation with

The North American Forum
on the Catechumenate

Acknowledgments

The *Forum Essay* series is a cooperative effort of The North American Forum on the Catechumenate and Liturgy Training Publications. The purpose of this series is to provide a forum for exploring issues emerging from the implementation of the order of Christian initiation and from the renewal of the practice of reconciliation in the Roman Catholic church.

Other titles in the series:

The Role of the Assembly in Christian Initiation
Catherine Vincie, RSHM

Eucharist as Sacrament of Initiation
Nathan D. Mitchell

On the Rite of Election
Rita Ferrone

Preaching the Rites of Christian Initiation
Jan Michael Joncas

Copyright © 1997, Archdiocese of Chicago: Liturgy Training Publications, 1800 North Hermitage Avenue, Chicago IL 60622-1101; 1-800-933-1800; fax 1-800-933-7094; e-mail orders@ltp.org. All rights reserved.

This *Forum Essay* was designed by Mary Bowers and typeset in Frutiger and Bembo by Mark Hollopeter. The cover design is by Barb Rohm. Audrey Novak Riley was the production editor. It was printed by BookCrafters in Chelsea, Michigan. Editors for the series are Victoria M. Tufano (Liturgy Training Publications) and Thomas H. Morris (The North American Forum on the Catechumenate).

Library of Congress Cataloging-in-Publications Data
Madigan, Shawn.
   Liturgical spirituality and the Rite of Christian initiation of adults/ Shawn Madigan.
     p.   cm. — (Forum essays; no. 5)
   Includes bibliographical references.
   ISBN 0-929650-80-8
   1. Catholic Church. Ordo initiationis Christianae adultorum.
2. Initiation rites — Religious aspects — Catholic Church. 3. Catholic Church — Liturgy. I. Title. II. Series.
BX2045.I55.M33   1997
264'.020813 — dc21   97-22387
                                          CIP

ISBN 0-929650-80-8
LITSPI

01 00 99 98 97   5 4 3 2 1

Contents

■

Introduction

■

Christian liturgical spirituality has a history of two thousand years. Christian initiation has a history just as long. In recent times, the liturgical renewal affirmed by Vatican II has led to a deeper appreciation of liturgical spirituality.[1] The liturgical renewal affirmed by Vatican II has also led to a renewal of Christian initiation.

The *Rite of Christian Initiation of Adults*[2] has provided a model of formation that has the potential for renewing the church. This rite represents a crucial restoration "in the way Roman Catholicism thinks about the whole of sacramental reality."[3] It is built upon a viewpoint that celebrates the all-embracing love of God as the milieu of human life. This is a shift from the view that looked upon sacraments as giving grace in an environment that was evil. The sacramental celebrations of the *Rite of Christian Initiation of Adults* do not make a formerly absent graciousness somehow appear. Rather, they empower humans to accept what has been given by God from the beginning.[4]

With this understanding of the *Rite of Christian Initiation of Adults,* this Forum Essay looks at the rites of Christian initiation as formative and expressive of a liturgical spirituality. The assumption of this book is that the *Rite of Christian Initiation of Adults* is a guide for the conversion and reception of those desiring full communion with the Catholic church. Because the experience of parishes in North America is that catechesis and formation are shared by unbaptized adults and baptized but uncatechized adults, the rites for both groups will be considered. It is also assumed that the rites of Christian initiation, like all Christian rites, form the entire community as well as those for whom they are directly intended.

Because the term "liturgical spirituality" will be used throughout the essay, the first chapter will define what is meant by it. There are as many shades of meaning in the term "liturgical spirituality" as there are painters of its description, but basically, liturgical spirituality is grounded in the paschal mystery. The paschal identity of the community is one of the mysteries expressed and formed through the celebration of liturgy. The celebration of the Lord's Supper is central to the community's growth in paschal identity. The breadth of the paschal mystery — the re-creation of the world in, with and through Christ — will provide a perspective from which to look at the conversion journey the *Rite of Christian Initiation of Adults* is guiding.[5]

There are many pastoral possibilities for adapting the rites that mediate and express the liturgical spirituality of the church. This essay offers some observations and suggestions about the rites of Christian initiation that flow from the perceptions of liturgical spirituality. These rites are a prime example of how liturgical rites can function as the church's school of spiritual formation.

It is the intent of this Forum Essay to invite further conversation on liturgical spirituality as formed and expressed in the rites of the *Rite of Christian Initiation of*

Adults. This essay is not a definitive work, but simply a conversation starter. Notes have intentionally been kept to a minimum, but occasional annotations have been added so that readers have a basis for judging which works they might wish to study further. A selected bibliography may be found at the end.

Sincere thanks are due to Hilary Haydn, OSB, for his willingness to share his valuable theological insights and pastoral experiences with initiation; to Thomas Morris, executive director of The North American Forum on the Catechumenate, for his creative scholarly suggestions; and to Vicky Tufano of Liturgy Training Publications for her editorial expertise. Each has helped to bring this essay from possibility into print so that the conversation can begin.

Liturgical Spirituality: Giving Thanks and Doing All in the Name of the Lord Jesus Christ

■

Christian liturgical spirituality has its basis in giving thanks always "in the name of the Lord." This grateful attitude is nourished and given direction by the community's liturgical celebrations.

Ritual celebration allows the assembly to glimpse the sacred promise of the messianic reign of Christ. People, bread, wine, oil, water and other symbols of the ordinary become mediators of the extraordinary, the new creation in our midst. Sacred rites make present the mystery of transformed reality in, with and through Christ. Yet the rites cannot be limited to a localized experience with the limits of time and place.

> Liturgy can never be a closed ritual. . . . Unless each member of the assembly lives the ritual moment in their daily lives, the content of the celebration is reduced.[1]

Although the rituals exist in a particular moment in time, they bring about an experience of eschatological longing that surpasses time. This longing, based on a

1

sense of the graciousness of Jesus Christ, does not remain passive within the individual or the community. Rather, it extends outward, drawing all creation toward the new creation that Jesus proclaimed. This, then, is the heart of liturgical spirituality: The belief that the personal and communal journey to the fullness of the reign of God has its origin in an experience of the intimacy and infinity of the paschal mystery, which engenders a deep gratitude.

In the chapters that follow, three questions will be asked about the rites of Christian initiation of adults, though they will not always be asked in the same order that they are presented in this chapter. These questions have to do with the use of the rite as a guide to spiritual formation, the model of church evoked by the rites, and the eschatological vision of these rites.

Guide for Spiritual Formation

The first question we will ask is, How can these rites be used to guide the conversion journey before, during and after the moment of celebration? The *Rite of Christian Initiation of Adults* is a conversion guide that can lead catechumens and candidates into this liturgical spirituality. By focusing on the mystery of giving thanks, the rites of Christian initiation foster a spirituality rooted in the liturgy.

> No matter what we say theologically, the faithful both learn and give expression to foundational beliefs through the community's public worship. . . . [I]n the very act itself of celebrating, meanings emerge that both confront and affirm the praying community.[2]

Good ritual is more than a time-limited celebration, for sacramental power flows over the walls of chronological time. The rites of Christian initiation are part of a longer conversion journey that spans the time before, during and after a particular rite. A well-constructed ritual will not be diminished by using some of its rhythmic invitations to conversion as a guide for spiritual direction before the communal celebration as well as after.[3]

The preparations of the "before" should enhance the "during" and flow over into the "after." This may seem to contradict the perspective that good ritual is most powerful without prior explanation. This perspective requires some refining.

Ritual symbols and the ritual itself do have power to trigger the religious imagination and memory of the community. There are, however, centuries of meaning that are part of the Christian religious imagination and memory. To claim that good ritual requires minimal preparation is true only to the extent that there is some religious memory bank that can be tapped through the ritual. The unbaptized and the uncatechized may have no access to this sacred memory bank, and their religious imagination may not be very highly developed.[4] Thus, some formative instruction "before" ritual celebration can enhance the "during" and "after."

Eschatological Element of the Paschal Mystery

The eschatological element of the paschal mystery raises a second question to be asked about the rites of Christian initiation. Before asking the question, some current theological perspectives of eschatology can help to set the context in which it will be addressed.

The Christ-event focused on in the paschal mystery is the basis for understanding the meaning of "eschaton" or "reign of God." The resurrection provides one basic symbol of the meaning of the eschaton, the ultimate future God has dreamed of for humanity from the beginning.

From the realization that God's promise of an ultimate fulfillment of the covenant is manifest now "through him, with him and in him," two questions emerge: What does the resurrection as symbol of the eschaton mean for me? What does it mean for all creation, and especially for humanity? The resurrection of Jesus Christ inaugurates a new sense of the present reign of God that opens out toward that ultimate embrace when Christ will be all in all.

Throughout Christian history there have been a variety of literalized metaphors of the eschaton, namely, purgatory, hell, heaven, particular judgments, general judgment and so on. Today's eschatology is not focused in the geography of otherworldly places and settings for judgment that the literalized metaphors suggested to medieval people. Rather, the eschaton today is a symbol that proclaims an absolute future of God anticipated in the resurrection of Jesus Christ. This future is a mystery. The communion of all humanity in Christ is a piece of the eschaton, but the eschaton has cosmic proportions as well. All creation will be made new as the love that is God's Spirit within and among the world's people bursts forth in humanity's fulfillment.[5] Vatican II provided similar perspectives on the nature of the eschaton. Although there was no one document on eschatology, eschatological reflections in several documents centered on the paschal mystery.

"By his incarnation, the Son of God has united himself in some fashion with everyone," and "the Holy Spirit, in a manner known only to God, offers to everyone the possibility of being associated with the paschal mystery" (*Gaudium et Spes,* 22). The inclusion of all people in the paschal mystery provides one interpretation of the resurrection as symbol of God's hope for humanity to be fulfilled at the eschaton.

The inclusiveness implied in the incarnation, death, resurrection and Pentecost events provide a hint of the content that Christian prayers and ritualizing should embrace. Ritual celebrations of the Christian community should expand the vision of the future in God that the symbol of eschaton suggests. The rites of Christian initiation are no exception. Because these rites are a source of spiritual direction for those being formed in the faith, it is particularly appropriate that the rites invite those who celebrate them into the eschatological horizon of the paschal mystery.

The eschatological horizons of the paschal mystery suggest a second question to be asked about the present rites: Is an inclusive Christian eschatology revealed in the particular rites?

Ecclesiology

A final question to be asked about the rites of initiation comes from the issue of ecclesiology, the understanding of church. The assumption is that a local church is a social construct and also a sacred construct that manifests what it means to be a community living with the gifts of the Spirit. The local church is the embodiment of a new way of being human, a new way of imagining and living the transformation of the paschal mystery. The community into which a person desiring full communion with the Roman Catholic church will be baptized will function according to some model of *ecclesia*. The rites that are celebrated will be both formative and expressive of that model or paradigm.[6]

Several models have been described in the past decade; their names are generally based on the way charisms are discerned. For the sake of simplicity, we will explore two of the major models. A mutuality or assembly-centered model of church is born of the communal discernment and ordering of charisms for the good of the community and the world. The priest-congregation model is born of a hierarchical discernment and ordering of charisms in which it is assumed that titles and charisms are synonymous.[7] Ritual expression of these models can be apparent in the manner in which rites are celebrated.[8] Both models have functioned in the church, often simultaneously.

The Assembly-Centered Model   The assembly-centered model is based on the egalitarianism of Christian initiation. "One faith," "one baptism," "one Lord," "one communion of equals in the one Lord" are all ways of describing an assembly-centered model. The many metaphors for the community found in the Gospel of John provide a basis for the assembly model, in which communion or mutuality is the basic symbol of Christian life. Whether vine and branches or the communion of humans with the Trinity, the community is based on love, which is an experience of God with us and for us.[9] Love frees people to be all that they are called to be. The creative unfolding of the person leads to the potential for deeper communion. The community of the baptized are the receivers, the discerners and the orderers of the gifts of the Spirit.

The mystagogical lectures of Saint Cyril of Jerusalem point to some perspectives of the assembly model. The egalitarian nature of the baptized is emphasized even though the order of the church of Cyril's time was clear.

> "Baptized into Christ" and "clothed with Christ," you have been shaped to the likeness of the Son of God (Galatians 3:27; Romans 8:29). For God . . . has "conformed us to the body of the glory" of Christ (Philippians 3:21). As partakers of Christ, therefore, you are rightly called "Christs," i.e., "anointed ones." . . . You became Christs by receiving the . . . Holy Spirit: everything has been wrought in you "likewise" because you are likenesses of Christ.[10]

The chrismation of which Cyril speaks seems to have been given in the imposition of hands as a sign of conveying priesthood, prophecy and royalty. Cyril affirms that chrism was prefigured in the anointing of Aaron by Moses, the anointing of Solomon as king and the anointing of the prophet Isaiah. This affirmation of Christian priesthood, leadership and prophecy shared by each baptized person was a familiar teaching for Christians of Cyril's time.[11]

Christians influenced by John Chrysostom understood that the Trinity was directly involved in their baptism. The priest was not the actor in the sacrament, nor was he identified as *in persona Christi*. The priest facilitated the action of the Trinity.

> For this reason, when the priest is baptizing, he does not say, "I baptize . . . " but " . . . is baptized in the name of the Father and of the Son and of the Holy Spirit." In this way he show that it is not he who baptizes but those whose names have been invoked.[12]

John's instruction encourages the newly baptized as well as the clergy to pray for the church because this is a Christian responsibility. Because baptism is a mystery of communion in Christ, baptismal gifts are given to each person. Thus, no one can look down upon another as if some had superior gifts. Citing Galatians 3:27, John affirms that "there is neither male nor female . . . no difference of age or nature, but every difference of honor is canceled out; there is one esteem for all, one gift."[13] He even likens Christ to a woman: "Just as a woman nurtures her offspring with her own blood and milk, so also Christ continuously nurtures with his own blood those whom he has begotten."[14]

The Priest-Congregation Model   In time, culture became a conditioner and a restrictor of ecclesial imagination. The plurality of models that had co-existed merged into a hierarchical model of church that mirrored the culture of the day. This movement is sketched briefly here.

The New Testament points out that communities gathered in the homes of women as well as of men for the celebration of the Lord's Supper.[15] Women were in charge of what was considered to be their domain, the house and its rituals. These rituals included the meals of the family and of guests.

There was no overall guide for the leadership of the Lord's Supper in the New Testament communities. Communal leadership followed what was religiously and culturally normative in each community. Who led the Lord's Supper was not an important issue for these communities, so there is little evidence to affirm or deny different roles for men and women. Because the household domain belonged to women, it is conceivable that they, as well as men, led the Lord's Supper in their own houses.[16]

As Christian worship moved from the house to the more public space of the basilica or meeting hall, the assembly model of worship changed to the male leader – congregation model of worship. In that cultural milieu, it was not proper for women to lead or to speak in public. Early historical documents show women who were about to be martyred, such as Perpetua of North Africa, speaking in public assemblies for their community. But by the fourth century, even this was considered improper.

Cultural practices, symbols and perspectives influenced ritual constructions of the expanding Christian communities. Eventually, as rituals evolved for the ordination of men, some symbols of baptism were borrowed and selectively reinterpreted, such as the chrismation, the laying on of hands, the act of clothing, the cup, and eventually the "character" that set the ordinand apart from the rest of the community.[17] The sacrament of orders, not baptism, was understood to offer the charism needed to discern and order the gifts of the Spirit.

By the early medieval period, the self-awareness of the people as equal sharers in the priesthood of Christ was overshadowed by a hierarchical sacerdotality. The re-emergence of the pseudo-Dionysian hierarchy, Scholastic reflections and the anthropology underlying feudal systems contributed to the eventual identification of the priest with Christ the high priest.

It is worth noting that the Council of Trent did not use this representational or identity language, although later magisterial teachings did. Trent's theology of priesthood was grounded in the same narrow understanding of eucharist that was essential to the medieval theology of orders and priesthood. Vatican II represented a shift from this approach.

Two Co-existing Models The priest-assembly model of worship has a long and evolving history that is still manifest today, albeit in a changing theological milieu. Vatican II defined priesthood as rooted in the person and mission of Christ continuing through the church. However, Vatican II did not resolve, theologically or practically, the relationships between the ministry of the baptized and the ministry of the ordained. The council recognized that the sacraments of initiation effect the participation of the baptized in the priesthood of Christ. At the same time, the council affirmed that the sacrament of orders belongs to the essential structure of the church, and that ordained clergy are different from other ministers.

Theological currents before and after Vatican II continue to influence theological perspectives of the ordained minister as one who represents Christ and the church. The renewal of pneumatology, ecclesiology and the theology of ministries has begun to shift the interpretation of the ordained minister as one identified with Christ in some exclusive manner. The diversification of ministries and ministers in today's global church provides a context for ongoing theological reflection on ordained ministries.

At the same time, there is a counter-trend to retain the cultural-theological constructs of the medieval world and the Council of Trent in spite of Vatican II. Priesthood is still tied first to the eucharist rather than to the church, which gives rise to an identity language that can still be found in occasional magisterial documents. For instance, a 1983 document states that a priest celebrating the eucharist "in a peculiar and sacramental way is completely the same as the 'high and eternal priest.'"[18]

Such perceptions tend to place more emphasis on the priesthood as the source of holy communion than on the community gathered. When eucharistic celebrations are more closely linked to an ordained priest than to an assembly, it is understandable that a document of our own day discussing how communities will continue to pray as the number of priests diminishes is named *Sunday Celebrations in the Absence of a Priest* instead of *Sunday Celebrations without Eucharist.*[19]

By contrast, the assembly-centered model of worship points to Christ as the only priest. All other "priestliness" belongs to the whole people of God as the Body of Christ. The priest is representative of the servant Christ in the midst of the people, but does not share in Christ's headship. It is only Christ who is the head.[20]

In an assembly model, the sacraments of initiation are central. Other sacraments are extensions. In this perception, the church baptizes into priesthood with as full a sacerdotality as the church possesses. Those who are ordered to a specific exercise of priesthood are not "more priestly" and the baptized "less priestly." There is one priestly ministry of the community that is in constant genesis at the baptismal font.[21]

The assembly model looks to the assembly as the locus of the holy, the church. The leaders of liturgy are the leaders of the assembly who exercise one of many diverse roles in the community at prayer.[22]

In the *Rite of Christian Initiation of Adults,* both models appear. There are times when the people claim their own role in the assembly. There are other times when the priest continues to take the part of the assembly even though "we" language is used.

From these reflections, a third question arises: In the rituals of the *Rite of Christian Initiation of Adults,* is it the priest-congregation model or the assembly-centered model that is acted out?

Liturgical Spirituality and Christian Initiation

If, as this book will argue, the rites of Christian initiation are a source of spiritual direction and formation, then the performance of the rites as well as the content of the words will influence this formation. The rites of Christian initiation can challenge a status quo, provide a temporary escape from a church in need of renewal or foster the coming of a renewed church in which the gifts of the spirit are expected to flourish.[23] Or they may do none of these things.

The chapters that follow will look at the liturgical spiritual direction that is possible through specific rites of Christian initiation. The three questions raised in this chapter will serve as one way to focus the material. Throughout, the rites of the *Rite of Christian Initiation of Adults* are considered to be both expressive and formative of paschal identity, a liturgical spirituality that enables all to give thanks always and to "do all in the name of the Lord Jesus Christ" (Colossians 3:17).

Chapter 2

Come and See: The Rites of Acceptance and Welcoming

■

Rabbi, where do you live?" "Come and see" (John 1:38). This exchange is part of the gospel reading for the Rite of Acceptance into the Order of Catechumens (RCIA, 41 ff.). It is fitting for the inquirers to hear the invitation to "come and see" as they begin the period of inquiry. This period is a "before" to the Rite of Acceptance and the Rite of Welcoming the Candidate (411 ff.).[1] It begins the process of formation into the sacred and creative memory of Christian tradition.

Five elements in the Rite of Acceptance and the Rite of Welcoming can be good conversion guides for the period of inquiry before the actual celebration. First, each inquirer is called by name. Second, each inquirer states what is hoped for from this particular faith community. Third, there is an invitation to hear the liturgical word. Fourth, the tradition of a communion beyond this time and place is introduced as part of the Christian story. Fifth, the gathered community promises to accompany

its potential new members on their journey to the celebration of the Easter mysteries.

Each of these elements can be used in many ways to
guide the inquirers during the period before the commitment to more conscious discipleship of the catechumenate. A few examples can illustrate how the ritual
elements might be used to guide the "before" of the Rite
of Acceptance and the Rite of Welcoming.

Called by Name

In some cultures, people are given a name at birth and, at
the end of their initiation, are given a new name that
matches their personal qualities. For some people, to
bestow a particular name is to bestow something of the
spirit of the person for whom one is named. For others,
a name is chosen before birth in the hope that the child
will develop a quality that the name suggests.

A theological and anthropological view of naming
can be part of the formative reflection of the inquirers.
At a gathering early in the period of inquiry, the inquirers can each say their name and offer some information
that provides a more personal understanding beyond the
name itself. Inquirers can be asked both relational and
creational questions. For example, are there family cus-
toms that account for your given name? Did any child-
hood names cease to be used when you got older? Why?
What meanings have you created and grown into that
accompany your name when it is said by your parents,
children, spouse, co-workers or friends? What do you
hope your name will mean when it is spoken or written
after you have died? If God called you by name this day,
what images do you think God would have of you?

Do you have favorite names for God, Jesus Christ or
the Spirit? What do these names reveal about your relationship to God? Are these names reflective of your own
personality?

Why do you suppose God wouldn't tell Moses a name when Moses asked? What is significant about Jesus naming us "not servants but friends" (John 15:13)? How is the name "Christian" like and unlike our other names? The responses to these questions can reveal a sense of God and self that will be helpful for the director of the group. Listening to the reflections of inquirers is one way to discover the sacred ground on which the inquirer stands. As the inquirers begin to verbalize their ideas and images of God, a new consciousness of their relationships with family and friends and with God may occur.

As part of this reflection on naming, biblical perspectives of naming can be introduced with appropriate initial catechesis about the word of God. Calling by name and sharing a name imply mutual commitment.[2] The relational nature of biblical naming, the responsibility and power that accompany knowing the name of God or God knowing our name can also be introduced. The inquirers might meditate upon and write about the mystery of their own names. As God calls them by name, what is happening? Are the inquirers being called to "come and see" something they have not seen before?

A simple ritual that links the person and name of the inquirer to God's person and name could be the reflective recitation of the sign of the cross. The words "In the name of the Father, and of the Son and of the Holy Spirit" with the gesture of making the cross are already a symbolic introduction to the paschal mystery. It is a shorthand presentation of a creed that will be explored more thoroughly at a later time. The reflective performance of this simple ritual can also instill a ritual consciousness of a relationship.

Hope

A second element found in both the Rite of Acceptance and the Rite of Welcoming is the inquirer's statement of what is asked of the community of faith. As the period of inquiry progresses, as inquirers share their story in the context of the Christian story, specific hopes can emerge and be named.

For example, suppose an inquirer hears Matthew 14:13–21 with a heart that has become aware that eating, by itself, is no longer satisfying. Even after a good meal, an unsatisfied hunger for something may remain. The compassion that fed and healed the people, that satisfied their longings, may also be the source of enlightenment that leads an inquirer to desire companions on the journey.

Another inquirer may be seeking life's deeper meaning as mid-life or some other experience reveals a need for commitment to something that will last. The story of the blind man in John 9:1–13, 28–38 may inspire this inquirer to name what is hoped for from the community — the light of Christ.

Other inquirers may simply wish to take an active part in a child's baptism or communion. A possible meaning of Matthew 2:13–15, 19–23, the self-sacrificing devotion of parents who love their child Jesus and the God of their ancestors, may not reveal itself until one's own child is to be sacramentally embraced by the community of faith.

Still other inquirers may have been inspired by the faith of a spouse or good friend. Or perhaps Paul's great hymn in praise of love, 1 Corinthians 13, has taken flesh in a spouse or friend in such an inviting way that the inquirer desires to draw from the same source of life.

Life stories contain as many reasons for inquiry as there are inquirers. In most cases, the reason will have something to do with another person. As the inquirers learn the Christian story, it becomes a context for their own story.

There is a reason one becomes an inquirer. That reason will have a link to what is hoped for from the community. As the inquirer identifies and names what is hoped for from the community, the paschal mystery becomes alive and tangible in a new way through the coming and seeing. The communal consciousness that the paschal mystery mediates is growing.

Invitation to the Word of God

A third element of the Rite of Acceptance and the Rite of Welcoming is the invitation to join the community in hearing the word of the Lord. Some catechesis about the word of the Lord can be introduced in the sessions on naming issues that have been discussed earlier.

Additional catechesis about God's word being a presence with and for the people can be generally introduced. The inquirer can be led to grasp the basic concept that God's word is not a book, but a life to be lived. The "word of God" is not fully God's word until it is alive and manifest in action. That God's word or revelation is spoken to a community and ideally is discerned in community is another basic theme that can be introduced.

One way to raise the consciousness of the inquirers about the living word of God is to have them name daily actions that might interiorize the living word. A daily examination of conscience on the living or non-living of the word could help the formation of the inquirer as a hearer of the word.

Prayerful possibilities of God's word can be introduced through the rituals that accompany the meetings of inquirers. The group might use scriptural blessings, psalms and canticles at the beginning and ending of sessions of inquiry.[3] Reflection upon portions of Sunday's liturgical texts may also be a possibility for daily prayer.

In time, the inquirers might also be introduced to some basic perceptions and different uses of "the word of the Lord" in Catholic Christian tradition. At this point in the process, the leader can point out that the word of the Lord was and is a humanly heard and interpreted word. The word of the Lord continues to be alive and revelatory because it is never completely heard or interpreted by any generation.

While it may be too soon to make fine distinctions grounded in exegetical principles, it is not too soon to introduce the concept that scripture is not intended to be interpreted literally. God's revelation to us is always interpreted in the context of our time and place in history. It is not God's word that is historically limited, but our hearing and interpretation of the word that limits the meaning. God's people have been aware of this from the beginning, which is why ongoing interpretation is part of the tradition.

Today, a renewed interest in possessing the whole truth and nothing but the truth has led to a fundamentalist approach to God's word. The movement toward literal interpretation that fundamentalism suggests can be pointed out to inquirers in a simple manner. Human words about God are metaphorical, revealing and concealing. Biblical words about God are also metaphorical. A scriptural metaphor, like any metaphor, ceases to be true when it is literalized. For instance, God is and is not like a father, a rock, a fortress. The reign of God is and is not like a farmer who goes out to sow seed, and so on. The point to be emphasized is that the mystery of God's revelation to humanity is greater than any one community's interpretation of it from their vantage point in history. The discerning community has some truth but not all truth. Those who believe they possess God or the whole truth are making themselves into an idol that has replaced the mystery of God.

As the inquirers become catechumens and candidates who attend liturgical gatherings, they will hear the phrase "The word of the Lord." It is never too soon to emphasize both the mystery of the meaning and the truth of partial hearings. In time, an introductory distinction between the biblical word of the Lord and the liturgical word of the Lord can be refined. For now, if the inquirers share their more spiritual interpretations of the biblical word, they will quickly find that people hear the lectionary in ways that are similar and different. This experience demonstrates clearly a living metaphor.

Communion

A fourth element of the Rite of Acceptance and the Rite of Welcoming is the community's promise to accompany their potential members on the conversion journey. The effects of this support will not be as strongly felt before the actual rite as they will be when the assembly gathers to celebrate the rite. However, the director can point out that the community at prayer is symbolized in each member's solitary prayer as well as in liturgical gatherings.

The solitary person's prayer, even though it seems uniquely personal, is still prayer with a communal foundation. Whenever a Christian prays, that prayer is uttered through the identity that comes as a member of the Body of Christ. The communal assumptions of John and Paul are worth noting here. The baptized are one community in Christ — no longer solitary individuals. Whatever is done has some effect upon the Body of Christ, member for member.

More importantly, the symbol of community in Christ that baptism affirms points to the obvious: A gathering of two or more united within the Body is a better revelatory symbol of communion than one who prays alone in Christ Jesus. Analogously, eating alone while remembering friends does not have the same life value as eating with friends. The analogy limps but the reality it suggests may need emphasis for some inquirers. The desire for **19** greater personal growth in holiness is always admirable, but the paschal mystery is at heart a communal reality. To understand and to become part of its meaning demands a willingness to become a communal person, a reality that many North Americans find challenging. The catechumenate will provide more time for exploration of the various meanings of communal prayer.

During the period of inquiry, the recitation of communal prayers, such as the sign of the cross, can be placed in this faith context. The responsibility to pray always and never to lose heart is a communal responsibility, but it is undertaken in both communal and personal forms.

Paschal Ecumenism

A fifth element of the Rite of Acceptance and the Rite of Welcoming expands the meaning of community. The family of Jesus includes the people of the first covenant, whose ancestral faith shaped his parents' faith and his own. The family of Christian faith is as large as the mystical Body of Christ. In time, the inquirers will learn that Catholic Christianity claims that the paschal mystery has "somehow touched the heart of everyone."[4] The paschal mystery reveals a breadth of God's love that may be difficult for inquirers to grasp. At the same time, the larger family of the mystical body is important to introduce, particularly for any inquirers who may have been influenced by fundamentalism, and may find it difficult to accept that breadth of interpretation of the paschal mystery.

The readings for the Rite of Acceptance provide good ground for the enlarged story. The story of Abraham and Sarah (Genesis 12:1–4), part of the ancestral tradition of Jesus, puts Christians in a posture of indebtedness to the Jewish tradition. The gospel read in the Rite of Acceptance is a joyful affirmation: "We have found the Messiah" (John 1:35–42). The "we" is part of a large family story with a past, a present and an eschatological future that contains a crowd beyond numbering. The paschal mystery has somehow touched the heart of everyone.

Although the catechumenal process is the time to enlarge any restrictive perceptions of God, Jesus Christ, church and sacraments, the period of inquiry can gently begin to present the paschal mystery as interpreted in Catholic Christian perspectives. The Christian story will be celebrated in the rites as a communal story that still continues as Christian memory extends the new creation into the future of God.

The five elements extracted from the Rite of Acceptance and the Rite of Welcoming provide an example of how rites can be used as a guide for spiritual direction. The "before" of the rite is intended to deepen the meaningful celebration of the "during." The rhythm of the actual celebration of the Rite of Acceptance and the Rite of Welcoming provides another dimension of spiritual experience and guidance.

The Rite of Acceptance and the Rite of Welcoming

The Rite of Acceptance and the Rite of Welcoming can occur whenever the inquirers seem ready for commitment to the catechumenate. The community, as well as the candidates and catechumens, is an integral part of the conversion experience of these rites. The three questions for analysis of the rites as guides for liturgical spirituality can be asked and developed here.

Guide for Spiritual Formation How can these rites be used to guide the conversion journey before, during and after the moment of celebration? The answer to the question of how they can be used as a guide for the   **21**

"before" period has already been answered. The question of how they can be used during the celebration will unfold throughout the reflections on the second and third questions.

Ecclesiology What model of communal celebration is found in the Rite of Acceptance and the Rite of Welcoming? Elements of both models, the assembly model and the priest-congregation model, are present. However, it is a simple matter to shift from a priest-congregation model to an assembly-centered model in the performance of the rites.

The Rite of Acceptance encourages "a group of the faithful" to gather with the inquirers outside or in the gathering area. However, in the text, it is only the priest and deacon who represent the church as they go to meet the assembled group. If the assembly-centered model is enacted, some members of the assembly should accompany the priest and deacon. In fact, it is already common practice in many places for the entire assembly to go to greet the inquirers. Why is such a practice valid as a model of church?

Note that the first ritual question asked in some form by the presider is not, "What do you ask of me?" but "What do you ask of the church?" Is a more inclusive symbol of "church" revealing for the potential new members? The inquirers are being invited into a church of many ministries and ministers. Consequently, some members of ministry groups in the assembly could be part of this initial welcoming.

The priest calls the inquirers by name. If there are additional members of the community accompanying the priest, they might ask the questions, "What do you ask of the church?" "What does faith offer you?"

The representative church group could then lead the assembled sponsors and inquirers into the worship space. From the beginning, the particular model of the community should be clear in the ritual celebrations of the *Rite of Christian Initiation of Adults*. Those who hope to be received into full communion with the church should experience the particular model of the local church they are expected to join. This conscious choice of models can aid in executing these rituals with integrity throughout the catechumenal process.

The Rite of Welcoming for the candidates begins inside the church, since these people are already numbered among the baptized. A similar greeting and unfolding of this ritual of naming, identifying hopes and declaring intent could follow the suggestions given for the Rite of Acceptance.

It is possible to celebrate the remainder of these two rites together while maintaining the distinction between catechumens and candidates. If the community chooses to embody an assembly model, there could be a rhythm of alternating leader and assembly roles. For example, in the declaration of intent, the presider could direct the opening paragraph (419 A), with the assembly asking the second question, which involves "us." Similarly, the affirmation, with its "we" language, could be said by the assembly (53).

Sponsors could invite their candidate forward for the signing, which would symbolize their accompaniment on the journey: "Come forward with me to receive the sign of your new way of life" (55 A). The signing of the candidate with the cross by presider, sponsors and catechist or director is an effective symbol of the whole church that accompanies these journeyers. If the sign of the cross was one of the daily prayers during the period of inquiry, the sign takes on a powerful communal meaning now that it is ritually connected to admission into the community (55 B). The closing "We ask this through Christ our Lord" of the concluding prayer could be said by all those who have done the signing, rather than by only the presider (57 A). After the signing of the candidates, the entire concluding prayer could also be said by presider, sponsors, catechist and assembly together after the invitation, "Let us pray" (424).

The catechumens and candidates listen to the word of the Lord with the community. The placement of the optional presentation of a book containing the gospels, after the readings and homily, makes a statement about hearing the word and receiving the word (64, 428). The promise to follow a gospel way of life suggests that the gospels will be a primary source of ongoing formation in the months and years ahead. The presentation of a Bible within the community is a teaching moment. It ritually says that the receiver hears the word within the community and bears a share of responsibility to discern meaning, so that there is both giving and receiving of the community's call to be a bearer of the tradition.

Because the community will hear the word proclaimed from the lectionary, the book presented at this rite often will be a lectionary rather than a Bible (note that although the heading over paragraph 64 says "Presentation of a Bible," the text itself says "a book containing the gospels"). In either case, the symbolic book serves as a tangible reminder that the catechumens and candidates are being called to deepen their ability to hear the word of the Lord and keep it.

From now on, the catechumens and candidates will take part in the Sunday liturgy of the word with the community. They will be initiated into the meanings of that word with and apart from the community. In a parish with an active catechumenate, the homilist must craft the homily to fit the needs of the mixed assembly.[5]

The assembly's formation is guided by the homiletic reflections as well as by active participation in the rites.[6] The presider at the Rites of Acceptance and Welcome can invite the community to do what those seeking full membership in the church are asked to do. All members of the assembly could silently say their name and identify what they hope for from this community of faith. All can be asked — as on Ash Wednesday — to repent and receive the gospel. The members of the assembly can take the name of a particular catechumen or candidate to support with prayer and encouragement. Members of the assembly can make a sign bearing the names of catechumens and candidates; this can be posted in the parish center or church vestibule to remind the community of their responsibility to be an example for these potential companions. During the Rite of Acceptance, the assembly could extend their hands with the presider in blessing as they recite the concluding prayers (67 B, 431). This communal gesture would underline the "we ask you" language of the prayer.

Eschatological Elements

A final question to be raised is that of eschatological perspectives in the Rite of Acceptance and the Rite of Welcoming. The printed text offers one way to assess whether there are hints of an inclusive eschatological imagination in the rites.

The first acceptance of the gospel has some optional addresses with different emphases. In addressing the catechumens, paragraph 52 A alludes to God's invitation to all people but then omits any reference to the community which has just received the catechumens. Paragraph 52 B does have a community context although it assumes the catechumens are only beginners in the spiritual life. Paragraph 52 C points to Jesus Christ but does not mention the community.

A hint of eschatological fullness could be brought into this rite with the inclusion of a simple phrase in the first address: "This is the way of faith along which Christ will lead you *and all people* in love toward eternal life. Are you prepared to begin this journey today" (52 A).

Other possibilities for eschatological fullness can be crafted into the petitions of the faithful and the petitions for catechumens and candidates. Well-written petitions catechise. Consequently, the petitions ought to present some of the breadth and depth of the paschal mystery, as well as its intimate power for the re-creation of the community. The suggested petitions are a localized version of an eschatological mystery (65, 430). The emphasis on catechumens and candidates is laudable, but the paschal mystery is a world-transforming mystery. That power should be invoked in the petitions that precede the celebration at the table.

The prayer over the catechumens might hint at an eschatology, depending upon how one interprets "company of the faithful" (66 A). A similar observation can be made about the interpretation of the prayer over the candidates, depending upon how one interprets "your people" and "your family" (431).

The prayers of the Rite of Acceptance and the Rite of Welcoming are clearly designed for catechumens and candidates, but in general these prayers are weak in eschatological religious imagination. The paschal mystery that has "somehow touched the heart of everyone" is a bit disguised in these rites.

Even so, the "during" of the Rite of Acceptance can have a powerful effect on those who inquired, "Rabbi, where do you live?" The church has ritually answered, "Come and see." In the "after," the period of the catechumenate, it can be hoped that the catechumens and candidates will find joy as they affirm, "We have found the Messiah."

Open Their Hearts to Understand the Gospel: Rites of the Period of the Catechumenate

■

The catechumenate is a period and a process that guides the catechumens and candidates "to open their hearts to understand the gospel" (RCIA, 93 C). During the extended period of the catechumenate, the catechumens and candidates are expected to witness to the gospel and to engage in meaningful prayer (75–105). To aid in this goal, the catechumenate utilizes the liturgical year, celebrations of the word, participation with the community in the liturgy of the word, appropriate catechesis, apostolic activity, the example of the faith community, the support of the chosen mentors and the rites of the catechumenate (75).

The *Rite of Christian Initiation of Adults* does not specify any length of time for the catechumenate, since the conversion process cannot be placed on a timetable. There is pastoral freedom to discern the most appropriate times for celebrating the various rites. "Nothing, therefore, can be settled *a priori*." (76) At the same time, there is an expectation that the period of catechumenate proper and the period of purification and enlightenment "should extend for at least one year of formation, instruction and probation" (Appendix III, U.S. National Statutes, 6).

This chapter focuses on some of the rites of the catechumenate: the minor exorcisms (90 – 94), the blessings (95 – 96), the presentation of the creed (157–162), the presentation of the Lord's prayer (178 –183) and the ephphetha rite (197–199). The inclusion of the last three, which may also be celebrated during the period of purification and enlightenment, is not a liturgical judgment as much as one that allows a possible flow of spiritual direction. The freedom allowed in the timing of these rites means that the director of Christian initiation can discern, with the catechumens, candidates and sponsors, when the rites will most effectively further the conversion process. Such pastoral judgments flow from the nature of the rites themselves.

Some of the rites belonging to the catechumenate are also appropriate for baptized adults desiring full communion (407). These include the presentations of the creed, the Lord's prayer and the gospel, the rite of sending the candidates for recognition by the bishop and for the call to continuing conversion, and the penitential rite or scrutiny. The rite of exorcism is not listed in the text as appropriate for baptized Christians.

The initiatory rites have been adapted and reinterpreted many times in Christian history; this continues in our own day as rites are adapted to meet the conditions of the present.[1] This chapter will place these rites in their historical context, if this seems necessary for analyzing the rite. The three questions — How can the ritual guide the "before," "during" and "after" of the conversion process? What model of ritual celebration governs the performance of the rite? and Do the rites reveal the eschatological fullness of the paschal mystery? — will be used to focus on the degree to which each rite is expressive and formative of a liturgical spirituality.

Minor Exorcisms

The minor exorcisms are prayers for liberation from evil through the power of the risen Christ. This power of Christ transforms the hearts and lives of the catechumens who are seeking full membership in the church. The minor exorcisms can be performed as appropriate during the period of the catechumenate (92).

The minor exorcisms differ from the scrutinies of Lent, which include exorcisms. The scrutinies are more elaborate rituals than the minor exorcisms, and they are not linked textually to baptism or to the pre-baptismal anointing, a point that will be discussed later in this chapter. Consequently, a pastoral judgment may be made by those responsible for the rite: Given the content of the texts, these minor exorcisms may be fitting for candidates for full communion as well as for catechumens. A brief history of exorcism may provide some context for making this pastoral judgment.

What is an exorcism? For many people in North America, the word "exorcism" means "sending away a devil." For many Christians, there has been a tendency to personify evil under the name of Satan, Lucifer, a devil or some other spirit. Although the scriptural texts about exorcisms are metaphorical expressions of evil, many Christians have literalized the metaphor.

Two perspectives are worth noting about the many exorcism stories of the New Testament. First, Christianity originated at a time when Jewish demonology had reached extensive elaboration. Demons were thought to be the cause of sickness as well as of good things. The exorcism-type miracles of Jesus are described within this thought pattern. Second, the point of the exorcism stories is not to teach that there are beings called devils.

The teaching point is that the transforming power of the risen Christ is stronger than the power of evil.

The story of the exorcism of the epileptic boy (Mark 9:14 – 29) illustrates these two perspectives. This account is a conflation of stories that became one in Mark's retelling. The intention of the story is revealed by its placement in the larger text as well as by the way the story is told. The story falls between two death and resurrection sayings of Jesus, predictions of his own death and resurrection (Mark 8:31, 35 – 37; 9:30 – 31). Note that in the telling, Jesus' confrontation with evil is overlaid with resurrection language: "He [the boy] is dead. . . . He rose up" (Mark 9:26 – 27).

For the early church, the tension between good and evil in the Body of Christ as well as in the world was cause for concern. Exorcism stories were reminders that the risen Christ remained present with and in the church to liberate it from its sinfulness. In times of discouragement over its own evil as well as the world's evil, the church prayed, like the father of the epileptic boy, "Help my unbelief." The church, as well as the world which God so loved, would be transformed in the days to come, if faith in the risen Christ remained steadfast. Evil would not triumph over the power of resurrection.[2]

It is interesting to note here that early baptismal rituals prayed for the catechumens to share in the power of the risen Christ. The rituals did not focus on anyone being literally rescued from the devil or spirits of evil. By the third century, however, initiation rituals began to incorporate some dramatic reflections on the struggle against the devil. These ritual reflections sparked the ecclesial imagination, which in turn inaugurated more complex rites of exorcism. In time, a formal renunciation of Satan and all his power made its way into the initiation rituals. Eventually the Western church dramatized and mimed a salvation history that ritually sent the devil out the "devil's door" of the church.[3]

Augustine's theory of original sin complemented the perception of demons and evil in general by assuming that humans were born into a situation of evil. This led to the view on the part of some that Adam's sinfulness had a greater hold on the human estate than Christ's graciousness. No more needs to be said here about the teaching of original sin and the corresponding perceptions of baptism.

In short, this literalizing of exorcism affected catechesis and ritual. Today, the meaning of the exorcisms might better be conveyed by a simple name change. In the *Rite of Christian Initiation of Adults,* exorcisms are prayers that ask for Christ's liberation to transform the weaknesses of the catechumens and candidates into strengths.

Guide for Spiritual Formation   Part of the "before" of a rite of exorcism could include reflection on personal and social sin. Discerning and naming personal evil and the ways that personal evil contributes to social sins or systemic evils can be part of the "before" of an exorcism. Such naming can aid the explicit invoking of power to transform one's life into a more authentic living of the gospel.

The mystery of God's presence and absence in a world that is not fully redeemed is difficult to discuss with catechumens and candidates. The death of Jesus Christ affirms that God's justice and reign have not come in fullness, but there is a hint of the coming of the reign of God insofar as Christ prays for forgiveness for those who do not know what they are doing. The power of God to transform creation is affirmed in the resurrection of Jesus Christ. The community that holds the memory of Jesus' resurrection and that is blessed with the Spirit can be a strong mediator of the power of Christ to confront personal and social evils with the strength of love and forgiveness. Humans can block these signs of the reign of God, however, by personal and communal acts that destroy or diminish the human spirit. **31**

The point not to be lost in all this is that the power of the risen Christ will overcome evil in the end. In the meantime, the transforming difference that a Christian community of memory can make in the world requires ongoing critical reflection by all members of the body. The power to effect the new creation in Christ is already inherent in the risen Christ and shared with the community. Well-constructed rites of exorcism can be formative of the religious imagination of the catechumens and candidates in this regard.

The prayers of the exorcism rites focus on personal transformation without reference to social transformation. The catechumens and their catechists are left to make the connection between the two. If this is not done, the personal focus of these prayers could foster an understanding of personal redemption that makes little connection to Christ's redemption of the whole world.

In spite of this, the "during" of the minor exorcisms can be a powerful moment for transformation of the catechumens and candidates. The moment can be enhanced by inviting the assembly to extend hands and join in the prayer over the catechumens and candidates.

The contents of the exorcism prayers are a mix of metaphors that could be confusing. There are still some relics of sending away a devil in actions such as breathing into the face of a candidate with the words, "By the breath of your mouth, O Lord, drive away the spirits of evil. Command them to depart, for your kingdom has come among us" (71). This optional part of the rite of acceptance contrasts with the earlier baptismal rituals that made no reference to spirits of evil.[4]

While many of the minor exorcisms are closer in spirit to more ancient baptismal prayers ("protect them from the spirit of greed, of lust and of pride," [94 D; see also 94 E, F, H, J, K]), some suggest a personified demon mentality ("free them from the snares and malice of Satan," [94 G; see also 94 I]). For cultures that retain a belief in evil spirits, the authors of the rite apparently believed that a direct naming of evils connected with false spirits was a helpful catechetical tool: "the worship of false gods and magic, witchcraft and dealings with the dead" (94 B). A few similar remnants of demon texts are retained in the scrutinies, which will be discussed at a later point.

The content of the exorcism rites makes it clear that the intent of the rite is to strengthen the catechumens and candidates so that they can be victorious in their personal struggles to live a more deeply committed Christian life. What is missing in the prayers is a formal recognition that the church and the world are also in need of exorcism. If the prayers could incorporate that vision, a more inclusive liturgical prayer model might result.

The prayers of exorcism could be used in many ways to guide the spiritual formation of catechumens and candidates after their celebration. At reflective points in morning and evening prayer, the catechumens and candidates could pray one of the prayers of exorcism for themselves, naming the weakness that Christ's strength can overcome. The catechumens and candidates could also expand the prayers of exorcism to include each other, the local assembly, the Christian church throughout the world and those who bring violence and destruction into the world. This adaptation could help overcome the mentality that separates solitary prayer from the eucharistic and universal prayer of the Body of Christ and help the catechumens come to the realization that the power of the resurrection is not only "for me" but "for all."

Eschatological Content Some hints of eschatological fullness occasionally make an appearance in the prayers ("May they work for peace and joyfully endure persecution and so come to share your kingdom," [94 D; see also 94 E, F, H, J, K]). For the most part, though, the prayers focus only on the present and not on the day when

God shall wipe every tear from our eyes. That eschatological focus could provide a more hopeful perspective
in which to place the "now" of transformation.

Blessings

In Jewish and Christian traditions, blessing has many
meanings. Blessing can be a form of praising or giving
thanks to God. The familiar prayer at the preparation of
the gifts, "Blessed are you, Lord God of all creation.
Through your goodness we have this bread (wine) to
offer . . ." is an example of this form of praise. Blessing
can also be an acknowledgment that someone is in close
union with God: "Blessed is the one who reveres the
Lord," Psalm 112 proclaims. Blessing can also be an invo-
cation of communion with God and the joy that ema-
nates from that communion. "May God bless you and
protect you" illustrates that meaning of blessing. The
gospels of Matthew and Luke have whole sections identified as beatitudes or blessings (Matthew 5:3–11; Luke
6:20–22). These blessings also serve as the revelation of
new commandments.

For the Jews, commandments are blessings because
their observance unites the Jew to the love and joy of
God. For Christians, it is similar: Whenever one lives the
commandment of Jesus to love, one is blessed. This new
law of communion in Christ is the blessing from which
all other blessings flow.

Source of Spiritual Formation   The Jewish and Christian
traditions have many blessings that are fitting for use by
catechumens as well as by those who will bless them at
other times. The beginning of each day can be a time
for the conscious blessing of God and oneself. God has
already blessed the waking person with a new day. The
person becomes that blessing by also awakening life in
others. Times of refreshment with food also can be times

of blessing. Times of work can be times of blessing. As the parade of people come in and out of our lives in the day, it is a simple matter to bless them at least interiorly. In the evening, as in the morning, there can be simple blessings of the night before sleep.

Eschatological Content Blessings are a form of praise and petition that reveal and bestow the power of the new creation in Christ. The Christian vision of the eschaton that is here, but not yet fully, suggests that blessings have a role to play in bringing the "not yet" into the "now." When Christians bless, they remember that God has already blessed all creation in Christ and continues to bless all people through the Spirit. Christian blessing is intended to affirm and strengthen the experience of the mystery of joyous communion in Christ that is beyond what we can hope or imagine. To be blessed is to enter more consciously into the love of God that surpasses knowledge.

In the order of Christian initiation, the blessings of the catechumens and candidates can occur in a variety of settings and as frequently as needed (95 – 96). These blessings are crafted with a variety of metaphors. The eschatological fullness of the paschal mystery is explicitly present in only one blessing: "Teach them through this time of preparation and enfold them within your church, so that they may share your holy mysteries both on earth and in heaven" (96 C). Two others hint at an eschatological fullness: "Prepare them for their rebirth in baptism . . . and the garment of incorruptible life" (96 E), and "Bring them into the fold of your church, there to receive the gift of eternal life" (96 G). Two others point to a possible universality of the invitation to blessing: "You proclaimed to all who draw near you" (96 B), and "You have sent your only Son, Jesus Christ, to free the world from falsehood" (96 D).

As a whole, the blessings are limited to those who desire communion with the church. Although this limited focus is understandable, the confined nature of the blessings does not further the paschal imagination that believes Jesus Christ somehow touches every heart.

Anointings

The anointing of the catechumens is intended to strengthen them (98–101, 103). In early Christian tradition, the rite of anointing, symbolizing the prayer for strengthening by the Spirit, was set in the context of an exorcism within a gathered community. The teacher laid hands on, prayed over and dismissed the catechumens from the assembly. "Whether the teacher is a cleric or a layman, let him act thus."[5] The ritual of anointing in the *Rite of Christian Initiation of Adults* has a similar purpose. It remains grounded in that context, with the Holy Spirit taking over one's own spirit of egotism, violence, injustice, or whatever needs to be healed, strengthened or overcome.

Model of Church It is curious that the *Rite of Christian Initiation of Adults* limits the performance of these anointings to a priest or deacon (98). It would appear that there is a confusion of these sacramentals with the baptismal anointings. The baptismal bath, the anointing with chrism and the laying on of hands leading to the eucharistic table are clearly in a different context from that in which the minor exorcism prayers and anointings take place.

There is a complicated history of varied meanings of "anointing" with the Spirit, a plurality of practices and symbolic interpretations of prebaptismal anointings and exorcisms, and a diversity of water baptism practices.[6] The National Statutes, which call for omitting the postbaptismal chrismation after adult baptism at the Easter Vigil, illustrate one theology of baptism and confirmation among a diversity of traditions (Appendix III, U.S. National Statutes, 16).

An early traditional distinction between the olive oil that was associated with prebaptismal exorcisms and the chrism or perfumed oil used for baptism remains (*Code of Canon Law*, canon 847, §1). Traditionally, the prebaptismal exorcisms were not confused with the sacrament of baptism. This explains the freedom of the catechist to do the exorcisms recorded in Hippolytus. Today, the anointing within the minor rites of exorcism is also linked to exorcism and not to sacramental baptism.

The tradition of Hippolytus that allowed the catechist to lay hands on, pray over and dismiss is still alive in the present legislation that allows the catechist to perform minor exorcisms and blessings (16, 41, 96). Anointing occurs within the context of reflection on the scriptures led by a catechist. Since this is not a baptismal anointing, why shouldn't the leader perform it?

Even if chrism rather than olive oil were used for the minor anointings, recent scholarship points out that lay anointing with chrism was part of an earlier Christian tradition. Lay anointing with chrism lasted at least until the Carolingian reforms (740–840 CE) that clericalized liturgical roles.[7] The bishop did have to bless the chrism, at least after the second council of Carthage in 390, but a priest or layman could anoint.

Today the catechist or other lay leader can be deputed to baptize (*Code of Canon Law*, canon 861, §2). If this is the case with sacramental baptism, performing nonbaptismal anointings in minor exorcism rituals does not seem extraordinary.

The diversity of ministries in the church can be a testimony to the model of a participative community in Christ. The less clericalization of non-clerical ministries, the better demonstration there can be of the community of church.

A different issue raised by some authors is centered on the trite texts of the exorcisms. The rich heritage of exorcism and anointing is reduced to a simple, generic **37** statement of strengthening, such as "We anoint you . . ." or "May Christ strengthen you. . . ." These prayers hardly capture the tension between the power of resurrection and the power of evil in its personal and particularized forms. Stronger texts are essential to capture the depth of the rite.[8]

Another issue emerges from the reference in the anointing prayer to "we" who anoint. The "we" is not the assembly, but seems to refer to an early baptismal formula that clearly indicated that the Trinity is the active agent in the transformation of the person.

Source of Spiritual Formation   The frequency of anointing as well as the context within which anointing occurs is left to the discernment of the director of Christian initiation. This anointing can take place in the context of a celebration of the word of God, as outlined in paragraphs 85 – 89 of the rite. It may also take place at a Sunday liturgy following the homily. Part of the "before" preparation for this ritual could be catechesis on the tradition of anointing as well as reflection upon the scriptural texts to be used during the rite. The anointing, set as it is within the context of exorcism, can be prepared for "before" by a sincere naming of the weaknesses or evils one wishes to overcome. During the actual ritual, a brief pause could allow the catechumens and candidates to name their weakness in silence before God or quietly to each other. The laying on of hands and the blessing could then follow.

The "after" possibilities for guidance inspired by these anointings could include daily reflections upon the realization of the prayer "deliver us from evil." The experience of liberation in Christ's resurrection can be extended and deepened through the use of phrases such as "The Lord is my light and my salvation," "Strengthen my heart to know your paths," or "Lord, be my helper and my deliverer" during private or group prayer.

Anticipated Rites: The Ephphetha and the Presentations

The ephphetha is a simple rite of prayer for openness to the gospel (199). The presentations of the creed and of the Lord's prayer each symbolize a reality of Christian faith and tradition. The basic beliefs summarized in the creed and the tradition of prayer summarized in the Our Father are foundational sources of unity among believers. The reception of these two symbols acknowledges that the catechumens and community can now walk together in a new way toward the eschaton. The creed and the Our Father symbolize the commitment of the baptized to live their profession of faith and to pray always without losing heart. In their longed-for baptism, the elect will make that same commitment.[9]

Before and After   The entire process of catechesis that the catechumens have undertaken has been their preparation for these rites. The catechumens could enhance their preparation through daily use of reflective prayers such as "I believe. Help my unbelief," or a phrase from the Lord's prayer: "Your kingdom come, your will be done." After the presentations of the creed and the Lord's prayer, thoughtful daily recitation at morning and evening could enhance the memory of the importance of these symbols of the faith of the church. In time, perhaps on Holy Saturday morning, the catechumens can be asked to recite these symbols of faith from memory. Many will already have memorized the prayers through their thoughtful recitation of them.

When to Celebrate   The ephphetha rite may be celebrated during the catechumenate. It can be repeated at intervals that seem appropriate to the director of Christian initiation. One fitting time may be the Sunday before the presentations, when they are celebrated before Lent.

This timing could heighten the importance of the presentations, as well as signify that the time of the catechumenate has brought about greater openness to the gospel. The ephphetha rite may also be part of the preparatory rites of Holy Saturday (79, 199, 104, 105). The presentations may be celebrated on a weekday of the third week of Lent and a weekday of the fifth week of Lent, respectively, if they were not celebrated previously.

The presentations of the creed and the Lord's prayer could be celebrated on the two Sundays before Ash Wednesday, rather than during Lent. One reason for this is the number of rites that are already part of the season of Lent. The liturgical integrity of the season ought to be enhanced, not obscured, by adding rites of Christian initiation. The communal nature of these liturgical prayers is another factor that makes Sunday an appropriate time for the presentations. Sunday is the day when the creed and Our Father are said by the entire faith community. Because the ritual presentations of these texts are as much about the faith community as they are about the catechumens, the community ought to be present at these rites; when they are celebrated on Lenten weekdays, as the rite suggests, this is less likely to be so.

The timing of the presentations must also match the maturity of the catechumens' growth in faith. For this reason, the two Sundays prior to the period of enlightenment and purification could be appropriate occasions for celebrating the presentations with those who are soon to become elect.

The suggested readings for each presentation assume that they will be celebrated on a Lenten weekday. The Sunday readings in the weeks before Lent, however, are quite fitting as well. These Sundays before Lent will be the sixth, seventh or eighth Sundays of the year. Note the themes of the readings of these Sundays.

Sixth Sunday of the Year
Year A
Sirach 15:15 – 20: Before you are set life and death.
1 Corinthians 2:6 –10: God revealed wisdom to us.
Matthew 5:17– 37: Your holiness must surpass that of the
scribes and Pharisees.

Year B
Leviticus 13:1– 2, 44 – 46: The unclean live outside the camp.
1 Corinthians 10:31—11:1: Do all for God's glory.
Mark 1:40 – 45: Jesus cures the leper, a sign of resurrection.

Year C
Jeremiah 17:5 – 8: Blessed are all who trust in the Lord.
1 Corinthians 15:12, 16 – 20: Christ is the first fruits.
Luke 6:17, 20 – 26: The Beatitudes.

Seventh Sunday of the Year
Year A
Leviticus 19:1– 2, 17–18: Be holy as I your God am holy.
1 Corinthians 3:16 – 23: All is yours because you are Christ's.
Luke 6:17– 23: Be holy as your Father . . . love your enemies.

Year B
Isaiah 43:18 –19, 21– 25: I wipe out offenses, forget sins.
2 Corinthians 1:18 – 22: God has sent the Spirit into our
hearts.
Mark 2:1–12: The community of friends lowers the paralytic.

Year C
1 Samuel 26:2, 7– 9, 12 –13, 22 – 23: The Lord rewards for
justice.
1 Corinthians 15:45 – 49: We bear likeness to the man of
heaven.
Luke 6:27– 38: Be compassionate as your heavenly Father is
compassionate.

Eighth Sunday of the Year
Year A
Isaiah 49:14 –15: I will never forget you.
1 Corinthians 4:1– 5: God brings all to light.
Matthew 6:24 – 34: Your Father knows all that you need.

Year B

> Hosea 2:16–17, 21–22: I will espouse you in fidelity.
> 2 Corinthians 3:1–6: You are a letter of Christ written in the
> Spirit.
> Mark 2:18–22: New wine should be poured into new wine-
> skins.

Year C

> Sirach 27:4–7: A tree's fruit reflects its care.
> 1 Corinthians 15:54–58: Thanks be to God for victory in
> Christ.
> Luke 6:39–45: A tree is known by its yield.

The generic nature of the prayers of the Rite of Presentation of the Creed (160–162) and the Lord's Prayer (178–183) allows them to fit easily into these Sundays of Ordinary Time. A slight adaptation of the Presentation of the Lord's Prayer can be made by the celebrant simply stating, "Jesus taught his disciples this prayer."

It should not be difficult for a homilist to link the texts of the Sundays with the intent of the presentations. The intercessory prayers may be crafted to include the themes of the day's texts.

Ecclesiology The rites of presentation assume a priest-congregation model of the community. However, there could be a more participative role for the assembly in the prayer over the catechumens. After the invitation, "Let us pray," the assembly could extend their hands and pray as the text suggests (161, 182).

Eschatological Elements Is there an eschatological fullness in these presentations? The eschatological fullness of the paschal mystery is expressed in the creed if one recites "I believe in . . . the communion of saints" with an imagination that fits the universality of the communion of saints. If the phrase suggests Christians but no others, then the understanding of the paschal fullness is still faulty. Similarly, if the phrase "Your kingdom come," is recited with an imagination befitting the comprehensiveness of the reign of God, there is an eschatological dimension to the paschal mystery contained in the prayer. If "kingdom" is restricted to "us," the paschal mystery has shrunk to tribal size.

Neither rite of presentation opens the fullness of the mystery clearly before the community. The crafters of the intercessory prayers may need to introduce the element of the eschaton into the prayers surrounding the actual rites of presentation.

Guide for Spiritual Formation   The rites that may be performed during the catechumenate provide rich possibilities for spiritual direction. Although this chapter has dealt with the rites as appropriate for catechumens, many directors of Christian initiation include all those desiring full membership in the rites of the catechumenate.

Each of the rites has the potential to "open their hearts to understand the gospel." Although it is the catechumens for whom the church prays, the assembly of the baptized can also be the object of the prayer. The community is always in need of opening their hearts anew to the gospel. By assisting at the rites of the catechumens, the assembly may hear the invitation of Ash Wednesday with new ears: "Repent and hear the good news."

Chapter 4

Guidance into the Memory: Rites of Sending, Election, Recognition and Scrutiny

■

The period of purification and enlightenment coincides with the season of Lent. Those desiring full communion with the church have been guided into the Christian memory during the period of the catechumenate. The weeks of Lent are a time for greater intensity of formation. The rites of this period are a vital part of the preparation for the Easter mysteries: the Rite of Sending (106–117), the Rite of Election (129–137), the Rite of Recognition of the Call to Continuing Conversion (450–458), the Scrutinies (150–156, 164–177) and the Penitential Rite (Scrutiny) for adults (459–472).

Since 1988, the rite of sending the catechumens and candidates for election and recognition, respectively, has become a popular adaptation of the *Rite of Christian Initiation of Adults* in the United States. Parishes usually celebrate this rite on the first Sunday of Lent (106–117, 530–546). On this Sunday, the parish community makes its judgment about the readiness of the catechumens and **45** candidates to celebrate the Easter mysteries. The ritual of sending the catechumens and candidates to the bishop for the Rite of Election and the Rite of Recognition of the Call to Continuing Conversion is an affirmation of the community's support of the continuing journey of the catechumens and candidates toward full membership in the church.

The scrutinies also guide the catechumens and candidates toward full membership in the Roman Catholic community. The scrutinies are celebrated on the third, fourth and fifth Sundays of Lent (141–146, 150–156). The Penitential Rite for Candidates (459–472) is the same in structure as the scrutinies.

This chapter will focus on the Rite of Sending for Election, the Rite of Election, the Rite of Recognition of the Call to Continuing Conversion and the Scrutinies, including the Penitential Rite for Baptized Adults. The three basic questions of how each rite can be a source of spiritual direction before, during and after its liturgical celebration, the model of church suggested by the rite and the inclusive eschatological horizon will be examined.

The Rite of Sending

The "before" of the Rite of Sending is all that has gone before this entrance into Lent. The months and perhaps years of preparation for the final experience of purification and enlightenment serve as remote preparation for this rite. A more proximate preparation can emerge for the catechumens and candidates in their consideration of the basic symbols of the Rites of Sending, of Election and of the Call to Continuing Conversion.

Source of Spiritual Formation Early in the process of conversion, the catechumens and candidates reflected on their names, their stories and the larger Christian story that contextualizes their journey. The community that welcomed them and accepted them has remained with them throughout the conversion journey, celebrating formal ritual moments as well as joining them in other experiences. In the Rite of Sending, the community remains with them as part of their unfolding faith and life story.

Catechumens could reflect on the meaning of "my name" and "our name"—Christian—by sharing together or writing their thoughts in their journals. After the years or months of growth, how has the meaning of "my life" and "our life" in, with and through Christ come to fruition? What difference will it make when "my story" is sacramentally integrated into "our continuing story" of life, death and resurrection in Christ Jesus?

The "during" of the Rite of Sending involves the community's discernment. Those responsible for guiding the catechumens and candidates will testify to their readiness. The catechumens and candidates will answer to their name and to their hope for full membership in the community, continuing the request made at the rites of acceptance and welcoming. The affirmation that the catechumens and candidates feel as the final blessing and sending occur renews their joy in this journey, a joy that leads to anticipation of the Rite of Election and the Rite of Call to Continuing Conversion.

The "after" of the Rite of Sending is also the "before" of the Rite of Election and the Call to Continuing Conversion. The spiritual leader of the catechumens and candidates can guide them by relating the texts and prayers of the Rite of Sending to the lifelong sending that the community continues to hear at every liturgical celebration. The Christian community, which is sent into the future of God, also has sent these potential full members of the community toward the future of God. Their journey into that future will continue ritually through the Rite of Election and the Rite of the Call to Con- **47** tinuing Conversion. The elements of naming, of personally witnessing to their desire and of being prayed for and blessed are symbolic reference points that have been consistent on their journey.

Model of Church The text of the Rite of Sending reflects a blend of both the priest-congregation and communal models of church. The degree to which there really is a community of discernment that can enter into the process of affirming the catechumens and candidates is a key issue. Many communities delegate the responsibility for critical religious formation to the clergy or other professionals. As with other rites, such as marriage and ordination, the community relies upon the judgment of those who have been the guides of the people who are presented for the sacraments. The Rite of Sending presumes that a broader group of people will have guided the journey of the catechumens and candidates. This broader group will offer testimony and affirmation on behalf of the catechumens and candidates, thus providing a basis for the community's decision.

Although the combined rites deal with the catechumens and candidates separately, and rightly so, they will be baptized or received into a community that ceases to maintain differences in title once they are full members. Whether one was baptized in infancy or adulthood, baptized in the Catholic church or received after having been baptized in another Christian communion makes no difference to one's status within the church once one has been received into full communion. With this in mind, a few minor adaptations of this and subsequent rites could help form cohesion among the members of the group while still maintaining the distinction between catechumens and candidates (537–542).

For example, a presentation of both catechumens and candidates could be simply made by the person(s) responsible for their guidance:

Father (name) and members of this community, these catechumens (names) are beginning their final preparation for initiation into the Catholic church. These candidates (names) are beginning their final period of preparation for reception into full communion with the Catholic church. Now they ask us to consider them ready to be sent for the Rite of Election and the Rite of Recognition of the Call to Continuing Conversion which will be celebrated (today) at (the cathedral) by Bishop (name).

To help us in discerning their readiness, I call forth the catechumens with their godparents and the candidates with their sponsors.

In the presentation in the rite (130) the model of church that is manifested is certainly priest-congregation. Although support is asked of the whole community (537), the address is to "Reverend Father." One would assume that the address should be both to the presider and to the community. Since the community already knows of its responsibility and will be asked a direct question in the rite, a brief form of address can be used by the presider to indicate the shared ministry of discernment that belongs to community, sponsors and godparents. This would ritually enhance the communal model of a discerning and participative community.

A more complete integration of the two rites than that proposed in appendix I of the rite (530 ff.) could be made with some simple adjustments that still maintain the distinction between catechumens and candidates. For example, the questioning of the godparents might be phrased, "This community has the responsibility of discerning the readiness of the catechumens and the candidates before we send them to the bishop for the Rites of Election and Recognition of the Call to Continuing Conversion. The godparents and sponsors of these catechumens and candidates have paid close attention to their formation. Now, I ask you, godparents and sponsors, do you see evidence of conversion of heart, formation into the gospel of Jesus Christ and a life that shows **49** a commitment to the worship and justice that animates the Christian way of life?"

If the number of catechumens and candidates is small, each godparent or sponsor could respond by saying, "(Name) has responded to the graciousness of God and taken (his/her) spiritual formation seriously. (She/He) is ready to be presented for the (Rite of Election/Rite of Recognition of the Call to Continuing Conversion)."

The presider might ask the assembly for its response to sending the catechumens and candidates to the bishop and for their willingness to be supportive of the catechumens and candidates: "You have heard the judgment of those who have worked closely with each of these catechumens and candidates. Do you add your approval to that of the godparents and sponsors?" (see 538, 541)

If the members of the assembly know the catechumens and candidates, the assembly could be asked for its testimony. This testimony, particularly from those who have been praying for the candidates and catechumens, provides an additional sign of community support.

After the approval of the community, the assembly could be asked, "Do you promise to accompany these catechumens and candidates with your prayer and support as they make their final preparations for the Easter mysteries?"

The address to the catechumens and candidates follows. The presider is the only one addressing the catechumens and candidates, so he need not announce that he is addressing them ("And now, my dear friends, I address you," 542). The presider can simply begin by saying, "Dear catechumens and candidates, you have heard your godparents and sponsors as well as this community speak in your favor. In Christ's name, the church accepts this testimony and sends you to the bishop for the Rite of Election and the Rite of the Call to Continuing Conversion" (see 542).

With the catechumens and their sponsors facing the assembly, the intercessions for catechumens, candidates, church and world can follow. The element of eschatological inclusion is missing in these prayers. If the catechumens and candidates are to be taught to pray with the mind and heart of Christ, these liturgical prayers ought to be as all-embracing as the paschal mystery.

It would not be difficult to open out some of the suggested petitions to the fullness of the community of the baptized. For instance, "That these catechumens and candidates [and all catechumens and candidates throughout the Christian communion] may be freed . . ." "That this community [and the Body of Christ throughout the world] may grow in the love that does justice . . ." and so on (543).

Similarly, the prayer over the catechumens and candidates could open them and the community into the wider horizon of Christ's love: "It is your will to establish everything in Christ and to draw us [and all people] into his all-embracing love . . ." (544).

Since the textual dismissal (545) uses "we" language, it would make sense to engage the "we." The current narrative instruction could be a blessing of the catechumens and candidates by presider and community together. The presider orders the action, "My dear friends, we send you forth on the road that leads to Easter." Then members of the community can extend their hands in blessing over the catechumens and candidates. "May you know Christ leading you as the Way, the Truth and the Life. May our prayers support you on the journey toward the new creation in its fullness. May you go forth to the Rite of Election and the Rite of the Call to Continuing Conversion with joy and peace. Amen" (see 545 A and B). As a catechist (or the godparents and sponsors, if the Rite of Sending is not part of a celebration of the eucharist) leads the catechumens and candidates out of the assembly, the assembly could applaud as a final sign of their supportive sending. Similar adaptations could be made as the assembly model of celebration becomes a conscious choice of **51** those responsible for the formation of the catechumens and candidates.

Eschatological Elements   While the eschatological horizon of the paschal mystery is essential to the formation of a Christian imagination in all rites, these final rites of the *Rite of Christian Initiation of Adults* especially should be crafted to emphasize the reconciliation of all creation in Christ. The Easter mysteries cannot be fully entered into unless such a horizon looms large in the hearts of all the faithful. This is particularly true for those who have been journeying toward the fullness of membership in the community.[1]

The Rite of Election and the Rite of Calling Candidates to Continuing Conversion

As stated previously, the "after" of the Rite of Sending is also a brief "before" for this rite. The elements of the "during" of this rite can be experienced more fully if the catechumens and candidates have reflected, in writing or discussion, on how the symbolic elements in this ritual relate to their whole journey. The basic symbols of name and community have already been discussed. Other symbols can be extracted as well.

The Rite of Election and the Rite of Calling Candidates to Continuing Conversion (129–137, 550–560 for combined rite) are usually celebrated on the First Sunday of Lent, with the bishop presiding. The biblical concept of election that is the basis of both of these rites provides the context for determining which adaptations may be appropriate within the rites.

The biblical notion of election is a corporate experience of God's call to "be holy as I the Lord your God am holy" (Leviticus 19:2). Election is a consciousness that God has summoned the community to do all that the Lord asks, a summons to holiness that implies continual conversion of heart. "To act justly, to love tenderly, to walk humbly with the Lord your God" (Micah 6:8) is one summary of being holy. To "love one another as I have loved you" and to "do this in memory of me" are New Testament summaries of Christian holiness.

One element to be made clear in discussion of the Rite of Election is the tension between the universal call to holiness and the eventual personal consciousness of the call. The elect are not inherently "worth more" to God. They have not elected God; God has first loved them. Once that election by God has been accepted, those who have done so are called "elect." Election is "about a God who leans toward humanity in spite of everything, a God whose love will not let us go."[2]

Ecclesiology The Rite of Election and the Call to Continuing Conversion are presided over by the bishop for two main reasons. First, election and continuing conversion imply a life of Christian communion and mission. Baptism celebrates the commitment of the believer to this mystery of Christ's body. Second, the bishop is a symbol of the communion and mission of the diocese in which the catechumens and candidates will exercise their full communion. The bishop is also a symbol of the larger communion of the Catholic church and the ecumenical church catholic.

As presider of the Rite of Election and the Call to Continuing Conversion, the bishop acts as a symbol of the Good Shepherd, whose mission is communion and whose communion implies mission. Consequently, this rite is not a time to focus upon symbols of triumphalism in the church. It is a time to celebrate the ongoing service of the Good Shepherd, whose mission is being carried out by his servants. Thus, these rites do not focus upon the bishop or the stately office signified by the miter. Rather it centers upon the servant mission of the church, whose shepherds carry the staff as reminder of their office.

Minor as these considerations of the bishop's clothing may seem, they are symbolic of a theological understanding of the diversity of gifts in the servant church. From beginning to end, the rite provides a subtle or not-so-subtle instruction on the model of community that dominates the church of the diocese represented by the bishop. Other elements in the rite will also foster some experienced model of church.

If the celebration has large numbers of catechumens and candidates, calling forth catechumens and candidates by parish is appropriate. The catechumens and candidates were already called by name when they were sent forth from their parishes.

When the call is given, the catechumens and sponsors may enter the sanctuary as a parish group, facing the assembly. If the catechumens are not in the sanctuary, they should at least stand within the assembly for the invitation and admission.

A slight correction to the text must be noted here. The parish community has not called the catechumens and candidates to the sacraments. Thus, it is inaccurate to say, "our community has decided to call them to the sacraments." As paragraph 112 states, "the community gladly recommends you to the bishop, who, in the name of Christ, will call you to the Easter sacraments." The bishop's address to the godparents thus requires some minor correction (552 A).

The godparents are asked to assess the readiness of the catechumens. A corporate response that names each catechumen can be said simultaneously by the godparents, such as, "(Name) has done this." The assembly should also be addressed, since they are part of the discerning community and will later respond to a direct question about support (552). A more direct question and response would be helpful at this point since the assembly responds that they are "ready to support" but not that they "will support."

The names of the catechumens may be brought forth as a symbol of enrollment. The bishop receives the names and declares the catechumens to be members of the elect in the name of the church. The issue of enrollment in a specific book has caused much discussion about the name of such a book as well as whether the candidates should have a comparable book for enrollment. The issue will not be debated here other than to remark that the scriptural concept of the Book of Life involves theologies of judgment and salvation (Exodus 32:32–33, Psalm 69:28, Luke 10:20, Philippians 4:3). The scriptural Book of Life suggests something different from the intent of a Book of the Elect.[3]

If directors of Christian initiation decide on two books, the Book of the Elect and the Book of the Candidates for Full Communion could be obvious names. These books could be ritually used in many ways as symbols of the ongoing power of the new creation in Christ. For example, they could be placed in proximity to the baptismal font or Easter candle during Lent and Eastertide, with a fitting "closing" on Pentecost.

The Rite of the Call to Continuing Conversion follows an order similar to that of the Rite of Election, with the exception that there is no bringing forward of the names of those desiring full communion. An act of recognition precedes the common intercessions for the candidates (and the elect, in the combined rite).

Eschatological Elements Although the prayers for the elect and the candidates are helpful as models (558), like most of the other intercessory prayers suggested by this rite, they lack an eschatological, universal element. The prayers over the elect and candidates are more inclusive and express the true nature of election as God's power (558). The second prayer could be more accurately inclusive if it read "to draw all people" and not just "us" into God's all-embracing love (559 B).

The rite offers two formularies for dismissing the elect if the eucharist is to follow; the rite presumes that the baptized candidates are not dismissed, although they often are in pastoral practice. If this rite takes place on the First Sunday of Lent, the solemn blessing for the day could be a very fitting blessing and dismissal.

> The Father of mercies has given us an example of unselfish love in the sufferings of his only Son. Through your service of God and neighbor may you receive countless blessings . . . . You believe that by his dying Christ destroyed death forever. May he give you everlasting life. . . . He humbled himself for our sake. May you follow in his example and share in his resurrection. . . . May almighty God bless you, the Father, the Son, and the Holy Spirit.[4]

The Scrutinies The Third, Fourth and Fifth Sundays of Lent provide the context for the celebration of the scrutinies. There is a separate penitential rite, also referred to as a "kind of scrutiny" (459), suggested for the Second Sunday of Lent. Only the elect are proper foci of the scrutinies celebrated on the Third, Fourth and Fifth Sundays of Lent.

Given the distinction, some identifiable differences would be expected in the content of prayer between the scrutinies and the penitential rite. The most observable differences are the basic symbolic referent of the Sunday, either the Transfiguration, the Samaritan woman, the man born blind or the raising of Lazarus. More subtly, the exorcism prayer of the scrutinies for the elect explicitly asks the elect to acknowledge their weaknesses and sins, to be cleansed from them and to be kept from evil through God's power (154 A, B). The prayer over the candidates desiring full communion asks for the same things (470 A, B), although the prayers for the baptized do not ask that they be freed from the power of the devil, since this presumably occurred at baptism. The intercessions acknowledge the baptism of the candidates (469) and the preparation for baptism of the elect (153). As the two groups move toward full membership at the Easter Vigil, constructing shared scrutiny rituals similar to the other cooperative rites is worth considering.

Source of Formation   The readings for each Sunday of Lent set the context for the prayers of the scrutinies, but it is important to avoid making the major figures in the texts analogous to those desiring baptism. The scrutinies focus upon the elect, but there are other conversion journeys in process, namely those of the candidates and the assembly.[5]

The readings for the three scrutiny Sundays are intended to provide a progressive movement from personal sin and conversion, to social sin and deliverance, to sin unto death and resurrection.[6] Exegetically, though, all the texts reflect the challenges of personal sin, social sin and sin unto death.

One example may clarify the point. The first scrutiny for the elect is celebrated on the Third Sunday of Lent. The three scripture readings for that day provide images of a grumbling people met with water in the desert, the love of God poured forth in our hearts through the Spirit, and the living water of Jesus Christ, experienced and promoted by the Samaritan woman at the well. The gospel was chosen to illustrate personal sin and conversion. Exegetically, the focus is Jesus Christ, the living water. Liturgically, the theme of living water for which all thirst is fitting for the season of Lent, the renewal of baptism and the Easter Vigil initiations. Insofar as personal sin prevents the communion of people, the elect, with all Christians, need to cry out in their thirst and beg for the living water.

Is personal sin symbolized by the Samaritan woman or the disciples who criticize Jesus for talking to the Samaritan woman? Is social sin at work in the mutual **57** scorn of Samaritans and Jews that the discussion about the Temple reveals? Where are the personal and social sins as both Jesus Christ and the Samaritan woman break the religious taboo of women and men talking together in a public place?

It is not personal sin that is the point of the text, but the power of Jesus Christ to be the living water, the new temple, and the one who dissolves barriers between Jews and Samaritans, men and women, and all people. John's community remembers the Samaritan woman for being an ideal missionary (probably to Samaria), who brought disciples to Jesus and not to herself.

The intended movements of the three scrutinies would seem better as catechetical tools if the integration of personal sin, social sin and sin unto death were unpacked each Sunday. As the season moves toward the Triduum, when personal sin, social sin and sin unto death will be ritually experienced and conquered through resurrection, the scrutinies could be wonderful teaching moments.

One dimension of this is the meaning that the word "exorcism" still suggests, and the need for catechesis on the meaning of this rite as one of prayer for liberation. In this context, some of the prayer language and images do not make any distinction between a metaphorical personification of evil and a specific person called Satan. The first scrutiny's prayers of exorcism name "the power of Satan" (154 A) and "Satan's crushing yoke" (154 B). The second scrutiny's exorcism personifies evil as the "father of lies" (168 A), and the "prince of darkness" (168 B). The third scrutiny's exorcisms also refer to the "spirit of evil" (175 A) and the "slavery of Satan" (175 B).

This may be more confusing than helpful. Contemporary accounts of demonic cults and Satan worship suggest that an emphasis on the power of the risen Christ over evil may be a more effective image than the satanic references. Those responsible for the catechetical formation of catechumens and candidates, including homilists, may need to clarify that personification is not person.[7] Sensitivity to the personification of evil as "prince of darkness" should also govern which texts are altered or omitted. The exorcisms need more careful crafting to be as liberating as the powerful love of Christ.

In general, the exorcisms of the *Rite of Christian Initiation of Adults* are true to the ancient pre-baptismal exorcisms. They are not about expelling a devil. Rather, the exorcisms are prayers for freeing the elect from the power of evil. The integrity of the scrutinies and exorcisms is manifest in the honest admission of sin in its many forms and the need for Christ's power of liberation (113–118, 164, 171–178).

Ecclesiology Insofar as the rite demonstrates a model of a participative community, the assembly could enter into the rite more directly. The leader could invite the assembly to join in the prayer and blessing of the elect and the candidates. The community as the agent of reconciliation, forgiveness and healing is an earlier church tradition than the "priest alone" model.

On each of the Sundays of the scrutinies, the elect and the candidates could be invited to kneel so that the community could pray over them in gesture as well as word. Given the structure of the exorcisms (154 A, 168, 175), the presider and the assembly can easily share the prayer, with acclamations inserted, emphasizing an assembly model of celebration. This additional participation can add to the assembly's experience of responsibility for the elect and the candidates.

Eschatological Element The eschatological dimensions of the paschal mystery that seems to be missing in so many other intercessions is also missing in the intercessions of the scrutinies. The elect and their godparents and families certainly ought to be subjects for interces-   **59**

sion, but there is a larger community with and for whom the elect should pray. Prayers for the candidates and their sponsors, for the assembly and the church, for the world's transformation and for all to be renewed through the power of Christ need expression.

Chapter 5

Easter Fire to Pentecostal Flame: Rites of Initiation and Mystagogy

■

Although the period from Holy Thursday to Pentecost is long, the nature of the mysteries celebrated during this period suggests that, rather than separating the Triduum from the Fifty Days of Easter, the whole should be considered.[1] This chapter will consider the liturgical guidance these days give to those who are completing preparations for the Easter sacraments, celebrating them and reflecting on them.

The three questions that have been used in prior chapters — the model of church, the eschatology and the spiritual guidance provided by the rites — will be discussed in an integrated way in the reflections on the rites so that the order of the rites can be maintained.

Triduum

The rites of Holy Thursday, Good Friday and Holy Saturday morning provide a final preparation for the celebra- **61** tion of the rites of Christian initiation at the Easter Vigil. Reflective preparation for the Triduum liturgies, as well as brief guided reflections after the dismissals on each day, can enhance the meaning of these days. The elect and the candidates, as well as the entire assembly, should be encouraged to take as much time as they can during these holy days to prepare for the Easter mysteries.

Guide for Spiritual Formation Holy Saturday, especially, is the time for the elect, candidates and their godparents. The preparatory rites prescribed for this day (185 – 209) may be an integral part of the parish's keeping of the Triduum. For example, morning prayer can incorporate the ephphetha and the recitation of the creed and Our Father (185 –199). The presider can introduce the eph-phetha rite as one of final preparation for the Easter mysteries, inviting the assembly to pray for the elect and for themselves that their hearts may be opened to the mystery of the passage from death to life. The elect can recite the creed as a group, or each person can say a few lines in the proper order. The assembly should respond with "Amen." The petitions of the day should include the preparation of the elect, the candidates and their godparents and sponsors among the other petitions for the renewal of the church and all the people for whom Christ died and rose again.

If possible, the elect, the candidates and their godpar-ents and sponsors should spend Holy Saturday in a rest-ful and peaceful retreat. Other members of the assembly can join them in prayer, especially those in the assembly who chose to pray for particular elect and candidates. Notes of support from these prayer partners and others, given after the morning prayer, is one way the commu-nity can show that they are accompanying them on this final preparatory day.

Holy Saturday is a day to be glad in the Lord. The day itself is a "before" for the Easter Vigil. The director of the elect and candidates can introduce the paschal mystery of this night in many ways. The mystery of the solidarity of all creation in Christ from the beginning of the creation mystery until the final "alleluia" of the eschaton will unfold at the Easter Vigil.

During the Easter Vigil itself, the journey from light to word to font to table will be the primary symbol through which the new creation's power is mediated. The richness of this night in which heaven is wedded to earth provides the main source for mystagogy, when the newly initiated unfold the resurrection experienced in the light, the font and the table. Although the fifty-day Easter season is an extended "during" in terms of unfolding the mystery of Easter, in chronological time it is "after."

This central time of the church year provides the primary source of spiritual direction for the whole congregation. The assembly needs care analogous to that which the elect and the candidates receive in terms of spiritual renewal. Fire, font and table are the mediators of the Easter mysteries for all, but like the newly initiated, the assembly will need guidance to explore and live those mysteries.

Eschatological Element The fifty-day Easter unfolds its mystery into the great eschatological vision of Pentecost. The opening up of the reign of God to people of all nations and tribes and tongues suggests the infinite number of people that the eschatological table will seat. The director of Christian initiation should be part of the liturgical preparations for the fifty days, so that the eschatological nature of the period is maintained.

Easter Fire and the Rites of Initiation

Though the Easter fire provides a dramatic introduction to the light of the risen Christ among the assembly, the great prayer of praise and thanksgiving is the climax of this night. The Triduum and the sacraments of initiation are intended to move the assembly with great joy to the climactic moment when all are joined in holy communion. It is a challenge to plan the Easter Vigil so that the focal story of bread and wine does not become a footnote.

The order of the liturgy need not be detailed here. After the liturgy of light and the liturgy of the word, the elect come to the baptismal font. The movement is accompanied by the litany of ancestors in the faith, a litany that can include saints bearing the same names as the elect and candidates. The assembly participates in this litany not only to invite the elect to the font, but also to indicate that they, too, are called to a new world of meaning through the waters.

The celebration of baptism begins with the blessing of water (571; references are to the combined rite of baptism and reception at the Easter Vigil). The blessing suggested for the Easter Vigil incorporates an interpreted typology that is catechetically minimalist. The rich metaphors of the readings are weakened by the blessing's literalization of the metaphors. Even the manifestation of God's powerful liberation, the wedding of heaven and earth symbolized by the lowering of the Easter candle into the water, a symbol that includes all creation, is not verbally expressed. The blessings of water that are suggested for times other than the Easter Vigil are more inclusive and also provide a participative role for the assembly (222 B, C). These blessings do not look back to the readings of the first testament but point forward to the eucharistic table, a welcome emphasis for the night of vigil.

A profession of faith and renunciation of sin precede the baptism. The renunciation of evil and the origin of the naming of Satan have already been discussed. The rites allow for cultural adaptation (238); an adaptation for North Americans could include two elements. First, a rejection of social sin or systemic evil in addition to personal sin and evil could be part of the renewal. This would verbally connect the renunciations with the scrutinies, which were intended to show a progression from personal sin to social sin to sin of the world. Second, the Christian conversion signified by baptism is not only about renunciation of evil, it is also about a conscious choice for discipleship. The passage from death to resurrection involves communion and mission, as the Rite of Election so clearly proclaimed at the beginning of Lent.

The renunciation formulas (573) call for the candidate to reject sin and evil, but social sin is not addressed. The second formula (573 B) is so focused on Satan that social and personal evil could appear buried under "the devil made me do it." It is easier to renounce all of Satan's works and empty promises than to renounce one's own evil.

After the baptism itself, a candle lit from the Easter candle is presented to the newly baptized. The prayer accompanying the presentation of the candle to the neophyte explicitly links these newly baptized children of light with "all the saints in the heavenly kingdom" (579), a nice eschatological touch.

After the assembly renews their baptismal promises, the newly baptized experience their community status by joining the assembly in the profession of faith. The assembly is then sprinkled with the waters of the font.

The candidates come forward to join the newly baptized for the celebration of reception into full communion (584 – 586). All are then confirmed. Inviting the godparents and sponsors to extend their hands in blessing as the presider lays on hands and prays for the coming of the Holy Spirit (590) is a fitting illustration of the ministries of the community.

After the anointing with chrism, the sign of peace is exchanged by all. The newest members might move to various parts of the worship space to exchange the sign of peace with the members of the assembly. This communal exchange of the sign of peace affirms that the newest members and the older members are one as they prepare to join in the great thanksgiving around the table of the Lord.

Before the climax of the Easter Vigil, some communities include a short break. A well-kept vigil takes time, and a break helps to restore and refocus the energy of the assembly.

If the assembly has left the worship space during the break, the ringing of bells to accompany a solemn entrance procession with the Easter candle, incense, newest members of the assembly and congregation can help announce the climactic nature of the great thanksgiving. "Eucharist completes the sacraments of initiation precisely because it establishes the church's identity and mission as sacrament of God's presence and sacrament of the world's destiny."[2]

The church travels toward the renewed life to be known in the breaking of bread. This night is different from every other because the church is renewed in the hope and the power of the risen Christ to continue being a transforming presence in the world. "The Vigil is a night of hard work wherein we undertake the construction of a new world and a new humanity."[3]

As the assembly receives the bread and wine, humanity rises again in the triumph of a new creation in Christ. This mystery opens out into the alleluia of the last days when Christ shall at last be all in all. This is the night when, once more, the risen Christ assures the church and the world that he has indeed risen and is with us still.

The joyful alleluias that ring out on this night will continue to ring out for the fifty-day celebration that is one day — the Great Easter. During this great Easter, from this night until Pentecost, the newest members of the church will be guided into the deeper meanings of the Easter mysteries. This period of reflection is called mystagogy, a name derived from the mysteries that have been received.

The eschatological vision of the paschal mystery has been well expressed ritually during the Easter Vigil. The inclusion of all creation in the alleluia song points to a model that might well serve as a basis for other Sunday celebrations throughout the liturgical year.

Easter's Fifty-Day Celebration: Mystagogy

During the Fifty Days, the Sunday liturgies provide a context in which the whole assembly can reflect upon the meanings of the Easter mysteries (244). Journeying to Pentecost and beyond, the newest members are now a vital part of the ongoing story of the church. Mystagogy unfolds in the guiding light of the texts and celebrations of the Easter Season. The liturgical celebration of each Sunday becomes the foundation for hearing and acting upon the word of the Lord.[4]

With the disciples of Easter, the newest members of the church can sing "alleluia," for they have seen the Lord in new ways during the sacraments of initiation. Thus, the sacraments of initiation are not so much an end as they are a new beginning for becoming immersed in paschal identity.

The spiritual direction of the new members during the Easter season opens religious imaginations into an eschatology that has its roots in the sacramental experience of the Easter Vigil. The early postbaptismal catecheses of Ambrose, Cyril of Jerusalem and John Chrysostom, preached on the successive Sundays of Easter, offer an eschatology that provides a soaring vision of the meaning of the Easter mysteries. Today's teachers can also guide the reflections on the Easter mystery into such eschatological horizons of what shall yet be when the day of the Lord comes in fullness. The fifty-day Easter, focused through the Sunday liturgies, is a time for integration and interiorization of the mystery of the risen Christ liberating all people (7, 37, 244, 245).

The liturgical use of fire, water, oil, bread and wine is one source for reflection upon the great paschal mystery of reconciliation of all things in Christ. Today, as in earlier periods of Christian formation, "the mystical meets the theoretical in a theology starting from experience."[5]

Starting from personal experience is necessary, but it requires direction and correction through contact with the community's religious experience. This is part of the task of mystagogical catechesis. The readings for Year A of the lectionary are suggested as the context for mystagogical catechesis. The Year B and C readings are also appropriate for this purpose. The scripture readings in all the cycles reflect the meaning of the power of resurrection for the ecclesial reception and use of the gifts of the Spirit.

The risen Christ as the great sacrament is the reality that integrates the entire liturgical year. The closer the new members of the church get to this great sacrament, the more their vision will expand into the cosmic dimensions of the paschal mystery. The more the assembly enters into the intimacy and infinity of the paschal mystery, the more the new creation will be brought into being in our time.

In a sense, a "mystagogy" has been in progress through God's graciousness from the beginning of creation. There have been signs of this graciousness all along the way for those with eyes to see. The baptized are privileged to have the doors to the sacred opened to them. Each Sunday of the Easter season, the celebration focuses on another perspective for which we are privileged to give thanks and praise.

The "during" and the "after" of the Easter mysteries point to the eschatological symbol of fullness, the fiftieth day, Pentecost. On this final unfolding of the Easter revelation, the church celebrates the many gifts of the Spirit that will renew the world.

Celebration of this day ought to mark the joyful end of the new beginning for the newly admitted members of the church. The morning of Pentecost could be a gala parish celebration of the Spirit that renews the face of the earth. It can be a fitting time for the newest members of the community to share with the assembly how they are beginning to use their gifts to transform the world.[6] It can also be a time for ministry leaders in the parish to identify how their ministries are expressing the mission of Christ. It might also be fitting to include them as planners of the Pentecost celebration.

An ecumenical evening service on the Vigil of Pentecost might provide a renewed eschatological symbol, one that has dimmed in recent years. As the disciples gathered in one place to receive the Spirit, the newest members of all Christian churches could gather in one place for an evening prayer of thanksgiving for one Lord, one faith, one baptism and a silent moment of sadness that one table is not yet possible.[7]

Any objections to an ecumenical gathering of this nature could be answered by pointing out that the Roman Catholic church has clearly recognized the action of the Holy Spirit in other Christian traditions. The Joint Lutheran – Roman Catholic Study Commission Report clearly affirms that the Holy Spirit "operates in the other church through its ministries and makes use of these as means of salvation in the proclamation of the gospel, the administration of the sacraments, and the leadership of congregations."[8]

This ecumenical setting for mystagogy may open up a dimension of the eschatological that can help the newest members of the assembly look beyond the boundaries of their own tradition to see the Body of Christ. The liturgical spirituality that can be awakened through this ecumenical celebration could expand the horizons of the heart so that all may find greater meaning in the priestly prayer of Christ that all may be one.

The rites of the *Rite of Christian Initiation of Adults* are bold in their potential for renewing the church in the world. The liturgical spirituality of the church can be mediated through these rites. The ecumenical nature of the paschal mystery that somehow touches the heart of everyone could be mediated more fully through some of the rites, and that is one reason why the church prays unceasingly, "Come, Holy Spirit" and "Come, Lord Jesus."

Conclusion

■

The *Rite of Christian Initiation of Adults* represents both a restoration and a promise. It is a restoration because its roots go back to an ancient formative tradition. It is also a promise that meaningful liturgical rites are a school of spiritual direction for the community. God's hope for humanity is mediated here and now as the community celebrates and grows into the mystery of its paschal identity.

That paschal identity is what the rites of the *Rite of Christian Initiation of Adults* are all about. The rites have been constructed to guide the conversion of those who wish to become full members of the Roman Catholic communion. This requires acceptance of the horizon of the paschal mystery so clearly set forth at Vatican II: The paschal mystery has somehow touched the heart of everyone, because the life, death and resurrection of Jesus Christ are "for you and for all."

The intimacy and infinity of this love of God poured forth in our hearts is at the root of the faith of the community. That paschal identity has a cosmic embrace that human imagination, even in its best moments, can only glimpse. At the same time, the rites that are celebrated here and now by local communities mediate that mystery and reveal its power to the hearts of the gathered assembly.

The rites of initiation bear a great responsibility for the ongoing formation of the church. They serve as guides throughout the journey, signs that both reveal and conceal the magnitude of the vocation to which the baptized commit themselves. The rites were constructed to be a source of enlightenment, purification, conversion and immersion into the paschal mystery. As such, they are a rich source of spiritual direction for the future members of the church.

These rites were also intended to be a source of conversion for the community. Consequently, the issues of the model of community that is fostered by ritual performance, the use of elements of the rites (before, during and after the celebration) as a mode of spiritual guidance, and the content of the prayers and readings are important elements.

This essay has used a methodology of questioning the content and performance of the rites of the *Rite of Christian Initiation of Adults.* The questions are one way to consider the nature of the spiritual direction that the rites can provide.

The critique of the rites was not intended to suggest directions for further development, but to indicate the kinds of care that must be taken if any liturgical rite is to present the paschal mystery in a way that can greet, meet and transform its participants. The experience of Christ is always a faith gift. But that experience can be enhanced by carefully setting the context for the mystery's unfolding.

The manner in which the *Rite of Christian Initiation of Adults* has been continually critiqued, renewed and reformed can be a good model for other liturgical reforms and renewals. For example, one adaptation has a definite ecumenical flavor: The assemblies of an Episcopal church and a Roman Catholic church joined together at the Easter Vigil with their respective catechumens to celebrate the service of light and the service of the word. A conscious baptismal communion was the ground of the communal celebration of this much of the vigil. The journey did not continue from font to table; the disciplines of both traditions would not permit it.

What if the eschatology suggested by the paschal mystery led to a different theological emphasis? Do all Christians really believe that the heavenly banquet table will be sectioned off by tribes of Christians? Will Jesus Christ appear and feed only some but not others because they lack something in Christian baptism? Ecumenical practices celebrating the one baptism and one Lord may influence the rites of Christian initiation more in the future than they do now. Even now, there are simple adaptations that ring with echoes we do not yet hear clearly.

The presentations of creed and Our Father bear their own surprises for the future. As people repeatedly acknowledge the communion of saints, what ecumenical horizon is suggested? As people repeatedly pray "Your kingdom come on earth as it is in heaven," what heavenly horizon is imagined? The formation provided and guided by the rites of the presentation suggests a broad eschatological vision that could be more direct and more precise.

As the paschal identity of the church grows in clarity, so does its eschatological horizon. The inclusiveness of the eschaton suggests a critical look at the kind of formative guidance some present rituals provide the community. What kind of Christ and what kind of community is suggested when the presider, symbolizing Christ the host, proceeds to consume the newly consecrated bread and wine first, while the people wait and eventually receive two-day or two-week-old hosts and no wine? **73**

What kind of sacramental theology emerges from the realization that a bride and groom give the sacrament of marriage to each other, but one or the other may not receive communion if they are not Catholic? To be united with the body of Christ in Christian marriage but not to receive the body of Christ in communion is a curious anomaly. It too says something about a governing eschatology that affects ecumenism.

The baptismal theology that guides the "before," "during" and "after" of the conversion journey of catechumens may raise many questions. If baptism is the affirmation of acceptance and openness to the gifts of the Spirit, which continue to be given to the church, can a church continue to predict who will receive certain gifts? As rites are celebrated with a growing eschatological perspective, will the divisions between people slowly give way to the power of the waters?

The model of pastoral care that led to a carefully plotted "before," "during" and "after" of the rites of Christian initiation is a model that has far-reaching possibilities for other liturgical rites. Formation and direction in every rite celebrated by the church can be made more effective with a clear "before," "during" and "after." For example, there can be a fitting rite of engagement celebrated as a "before" to marriage. A rite repeated during pregnancy can be a "before" celebration of the birth of a child. The blessing of the room or the bed that will be the child's can serve as a ritual reminder that potentially all space in which love is manifest is holy space.

The rites of the *Rite of Christian Initiation of Adults* make it clear that there is need for ongoing formation and direction of the entire local community as well as of the individuals desiring communion with the church. The rites are structured to invite additional participation so that all the members of the community can enter into these rites with greater awareness of their meaning and potential for conversion.

What if this were true of all other rites? What if a model of the assembly were intentionally written into the performance of the rites? How would the present rites for the anointing of the sick change if the principles were applied? How could the person who is ill be called upon to bless those who are mourning so that the community's faith could be strengthened? It is not only the newly baptized who can give testimony to faith during the Easter season. There may be many who can bear testimony to the amazing grace that enables them to accept death, which transforms even as it diminishes vitality, as the final revealer of life.

The rites of Christian initiation use the texts of the lectionary as a guide for those desiring full membership in the church. Creative catechists and directors of Christian initiation have used journal-keeping and other forms of active involvement to keep the word of the Lord alive in the lives of the seekers. Dialogue between homilists and catechists could be an asset to both as they consider the conversion of seekers and assembly.

Those who seek full communion with the church are invited week after week to become part of a community that is free to share its growing faith. There is an expectation that the larger faith community does this all the time. Is there a way to assist the larger community to do faith-sharing within the many rites of the community? If not, will the newly baptized really fit or be formed in an ongoing way through community ritual?

The renewal of the rites of the *Rite of Christian Initiation of Adults* was not intended to serve as a model for further renewal of every other rite of the Roman church. Yet, this process, if well enacted, can and does affect other rites. Consider how the reflections of The North American Forum on the Catechumenate have enhanced the theological and pastoral implications of the ongoing revisions. The consistent discussions have led to a richness of ritual that is still unfolding. What if each rite celebrated by the church had a comparable national group of pastors, theologians, catechists and liturgists who met regularly to consider its ongoing evolution? Would a new awareness of the dearth of ritual meaning for young adults result in expanded ritual possibilities? Would a quicker pace for the renewal of the church ensue? Would ecumenism be more than a word?

The *Rite of Christian Initiation of Adults* has opened up a new liturgical spirituality for the church. The journey from inquiry to assembly to font to table to Pentecostal vision of the eschaton has an integrity in the rites. The fact that these rites are similar to rites of initiation across Christian communions points to many exciting possibilities, not least of which is the action that may someday be a visible sign of the communion into which we have been baptized.

Out of an eschatological vision that approaches the intimacy and infinity of the paschal mystery, there will be a new church. The divisions of Roman, Lutheran, Episcopalian, Methodist and all other Christians may not cease to be, but they will begin to realize that the Lord's table is the Lord's, and not any one group's sole possession. The infinite embrace of the paschal mystery will then be seen as the all-inclusive reality that it is.

This journey from font to table to eschaton has been given direction in the rites of the *Rite of Christian Initiation of Adults.* Its potential for renewing the church and the face of the earth has only just begun. That is why the conversation must continue!

Notes

Introduction

[1] A history and a critique of some of the literature can be found in James Dallen, "Liturgical Spirituality: Living What We Sing About," *Liturgical Ministry* 4 (Spring, 1995) pp. 49–59; see also Kevin Irwin, *Liturgy, Prayer and Spirituality* (New York: Paulist, 1984); Shawn Madigan, C.S.J., "Spirituality, liturgical," *The New Dictionary of Sacramental Worship,* ed. Peter E. Fink (Collegeville: Liturgical Press, 1990), pp. 1224–1231; Joyce Ann Zimmerman, C.PP.S., *Liturgy as Living Faith: A Liturgical Spirituality* (Scranton: University of Scranton Press, 1993).

[2] All references to the *Rite of Christian Initiation of Adults* come from the 1988 edition approved by the U.S. National Conference of Catholic Bishops and confirmed by the Apostolic See for use in the dioceses of the United States.

[3] Aidan Kavanagh, *The Shape of Baptism: The Rite of Christian Initiation* (New York: Pueblo, 1978). For a concise summary of the conciliar reforms and the evolution of the *Rite of Christian Initiation of Adults,* see pp. 81–126.

[4] Tad Guzie, "Theological Challenges," in *Becoming a Catholic Christian: A Symposium on Christian Initiation,* ed. William J. Reedy (New York: Sadlier, 1975), pp. 165–173.

[5] Nathan D. Mitchell has developed this perspective well in his *Eucharist as Sacrament of Initiation,* Forum Essays, No. 2 (Chicago: Liturgy Training Publications, 1994), especially pp. 47–114.

Chapter 1

[1] Joyce Ann Zimmerman, C.P.P.S., "Liturgical Assembly: Who Is the Subject of Liturgy?" *Liturgical Ministry,* Vol. 3 (Spring, 1994): p. 51.

[2] Thomas H. Morris, "Ministry: Response to Baptismal Call," *Liturgical Ministry,* Vol. 3 (Spring, 1994): p. 60.

[3] Thomas H. Morris has used this sacramental approach in his helpful and critical resource work on Christian initiation, *The RCIA Transforming the Church: A Resource for Pastoral Implementation* (New York: Paulist, 1989).

[4] Mary Collins, O.S.B., *Worship: Renewal to Practice* (Washington: Pastoral Press, 1987), pp. 265–276.

[5] Zachary Hayes, *Visions of a Future: A Study of Christian Eschatology* (Wilmington: Michael Glazier, 1989); Karl Rahner, "The Life of the Dead," *More Recent Theological Writings,* Theological Investigations 4, trans. K. Smyth (New York: Seabury, 1974), pp. 347–354; Michael Morrissey, "Afterlife," *The New Dictionary of*

Catholic Spirituality, ed. Michael Downey (Collegeville: Liturgical Press, 1993), pp. 24–30.

6 Michael Warren, "Speaking and Learning in the Local Church: A Look at the Material Conditions," *Worship,* 69:1 (January, 1995), pp. 28–50.

7 The two models compared here are drawn from Bob Hurd, "Liturgy and Empowerment: The Restoration of the Liturgical Assembly," in *That They Might Live: Power, Empowerment and Leadership in the Church,* ed. Michael Downey (New York: Crossroad, 1991), pp. 130–155.

8 *Mysticism and the Institutional Crisis,* Concilium 1994/4, ed. Christian Duquoc and Gustavo Gutierrez (Maryknoll: Orbis, 1994), pp. 17–27, 59–80, 91–106; Yves Congar, "The Historical Development of Authority," in *Problems of Authority,* ed. John Murray Todd (Baltimore: Helicon, 1962), pp. 140–156.

9 Catherine Mowry LaCugna, *God for Us: The Trinity and Christian Life* (San Francisco: HarperSanFrancisco, 1991); a more focused version of this is "God in Communion with Us," in *Freeing Theology* (San Francisco: HarperSanFrancisco, 1993), pp. 83–114; see also Elizabeth A. Johnson, *She Who Is* (New York: Crossroad, 1994), pp. 191–223.

10 "The Holy Chrism," Third Lecture on the Mysteries, in *The Works of Saint Cyril of Jerusalem,* vol. 2, trans. Leo P. McCauley, SJ, and Anthony A. Stephenson (Washington: The Catholic University of America, 1970), pp. 168–169. This is from *The Fathers of the Church* series, vol. 64, ed. dir., Bernard M. Peebles.

11 These elements are clearly present in Cyril's mystagogical lectures (op. cit., 3:6, pp. 168–173; 7:44, p. 180). Though typology is not the exegetical approach used today, the concepts conveyed are similar to elements of the baptismal ritual.

12 Saint John Chrysostom, "Baptismal Instructions," translated and annotated by Paul W. Harkens (Westminster: Newman Press, 1963), p. 165.

13 John Chrysostom, op. cit., "The Eleventh Instruction," 11:21, p. 167.

14 John Chrysostom, op. cit., "The Third Instruction," 3:19, p. 62. The importance of imaging Christ was one reason John forbade women to wear cosmetics. The Creator's design of inner beauty should not be confused with outer beauty (op. cit., "The First Instruction," 1:34–38, pp. 36–39).

15 Acts 12:12–17, 16:15, 18:2; Colossians 4:15; Philemon 2; 1 Corinthians 16:19; Romans 16:1–6 are but a few texts that point to the exercise of charisms of leadership in the early church.

16 Ben Witherington III, *Women in the Earliest Churches* (New York: Cambridge University Press, 1988); Ross Shepard Kraemer, *Her Share of the Blessings* (New York: Oxford University Press, 1992), pp. 128–190; Neil Elliott, *Liberating Paul* (Maryknoll: Orbis, 1994), pp. 31–54.

17 See David Power, *Ministers of Christ and His Church* (London: G. Chapman, 1969); Gerard Ellard, SJ, *Ordination Anointings in the Western Church Before 1000 AD* (Cambridge, MA:

The Medieval Academy of America, 1933); Mary Collins, OSB, *Worship: Renewal to Practice* (Washington: Pastoral Press, 1986); Nathan Mitchell, *Mission and Ministry* (Wilmington: Michael Glazier, 1982); Patrick McGoldrick, "Orders," in *The New Dictionary of Sacramental Worship,* ed. Peter J. Fink, SJ, (Collegeville: Liturgical Press, 1990), pp. 896 – 908.

[18] "Letter of the Congregation for the Doctrine of the Faith on the Subject of the Role of Ordained Ministry of the Episcopate and Presbyterate in the Celebration of the Eucharist, Aug. 6, 1983," *AAS* 75 (1983), p. 1006.

[19] James Dallen has discussed implications of this in his scholarly work, *The Dilemma of Priestless Sundays* (Chicago: Liturgy Training Publications, 1994).

[20] Dennis Michael Ferrara has developed issues of priestly identity in "*In Persona Christi:* Toward a Second Naivete," *Theological Studies* 57 (1996), pp. 65 – 88.

[21] Aidan Kavanagh, "Unfinished and Unbegun Revisited: The Rite of Christian Initiation of Adults," in *Living Water, Sealing Spirit: Readings in Christian Initiation,* ed. Maxwell Johnson (Collegeville: Liturgical Press/Pueblo, 1995), pp. 259 – 273.

[22] A readable basic summary of the development of this model can be found in James D. Whitehead, "Christian Images of Community: Power and Leadership," in *Leadership Ministry in Community,* ed. Michael A. Cowan, *Alternative Futures for Worship,* Vol. 6 (Collegeville: Liturgical Press, 1987), pp. 23 – 37.

[23] Catherine Vincie has examined this in "Gender Analysis and Christian Initiation," *Worship,* 69:6 (November, 1995), pp. 505 – 530.

Chapter 2

[1] Some prefer the combined rite, "Celebration of the Rite of Acceptance into the Order of Catechumens and of the Rite of Welcoming Baptized but Previously Uncatechized Adults who are Preparing for Confirmation and/or Eucharist or Reception into the Full Communion of the Catholic Church," for use when celebrating with both unbaptized and baptized candidates. The combined rite contains the same basic elements found in the two separate rites. See *RCIA,* Appendix I, 505 – 529.

[2] See Isaiah 43; Jeremiah 1; John 13, 15:15, 17; 1 John 4:7–21.

[3] See, for example, 2 Corinthians 1:2 – 4, 13:13; Ephesians 1:2 – 6, 3:16 – 21.

[4] *Gaudium et Spes,* 22.

[5] The possibilities have been discussed by Jan Michael Joncas, *Preaching the Rites of Christian Initiation,* Forum Essays, No. 4 (Chicago: Liturgy Training Publications, 1994).

[6] Catherine Dooley refers to liturgical participation as one mode of liturgical catechesis in her detailed development of liturgical catechesis. See Catherine Dooley, "Liturgical Catechesis: Mystagogy, Marriage or Misnomer," *Worship* 66:5 (September 1992), pp. 386 – 397.

Chapter 3

[1] Leonel L. Mitchell, *Worship: Initiation and the Churches* (Washington: Pastoral Press, 1991), pp. 149.

[2] John R. Donahue, "Mark," in *Harper's Bible Commentary,* ed. James L. Mays (San Francisco: Harper and Row, 1988), pp. 983 – 985, 995; also see C. S. Mann, *Mark* (Garden City, NY: Doubleday, 1986), pp. 214 – 218.

[3] Henry Ansgar Kelly, *The Devil at Baptism: Ritual, Theology, and Drama* (Ithaca: Cornell University Press, 1985), pp. 1– 56, 262 – 277.

[4] Robert D. Duggan discusses this in "Conversion in the *Ordo initiationis Christianae adultorum,*" *Ephemerides liturgicae* 96 (1982), pp. 57– 83, 209 – 252, and in the following issue 97 (1983), pp. 141– 233.

[5] Hippolytus, *The Apostolic Tradition,* translation and commentary by Geoffrey J. Cuming, in *Hippolytus: A Text for Students* (Long Easton, Nottingham: Hassell and Lucking, 1976), p. 19.

[6] Gabriele Winkler, "The Original Meaning of the Pre-baptismal Anointing and Its Implications," *Living Water, Sealing Spirit,* pp. 58 – 81.

[7] John J. Ziegler, "Who Can Anoint the Sick?" *Worship* 61:1 (January 1987), pp. 25 – 44.

[8] Gerard Austin, "Anointing with the Oil of Catechumens," *Catechumenate: A Journal of Christian Initiation,* (September 1987), pp. 2 –10.

[9] Aidan Kavanagh, "The Presentations: Creed and Lord's Prayer," *Catechumenate: A Journal of Christian Initiation* (July 1987), pp. 2 – 8.

Chapter 4

[1] E. Byron Anderson, "Performance, Practice and Meaning in Christian Baptism," *Worship,* 69:6 (November 1995), pp. 482 -504.

[2] Rita Ferrone, *On the Rite of Election,* Forum Essays, No. 3 (Chicago: Liturgy Training Publications, 1994), p. 55. This is a readable discussion of the historical and ritual setting for the Rite of Election.

[3] See Ferrone, pp. 77– 84.

[4] The *Sacramentary* (New York: Catholic Book Publishing Co., 1985), p. 83.

[5] Jan Michael Joncas has treated this in *Preaching the Rites of Christian Initiation,* pp. 23 – 94.

[6] The three scrutinies are examined in *Commentaries: Rite of Christian Initiation of Adults,* ed. James A. Wilde (Chicago: Liturgy Training Publications, 1988). See Robert D. Duggan, "Coming to Know Jesus the Christ: The First Scrutiny," pp. 43 – 51; "God Towers Over Evil: The Second Scrutiny," pp. 53 – 60; Mark Searle, "For the Glory of God: The Third Scrutiny," pp. 61–72.

[7] Any current biblical commentary does this well. For example, see *The New Jerome Biblical Commentary,* ed. Raymond E. Brown, Joseph A. Fitzmyer and Roland E. Murphy (Englewood Cliffs: Prentice Hall, 1990), 41:6, 23; 43:177; 44:37; 46:25; 49:29, 35; 50:50, 55; 51:134; 53:20; 55:5 passim.

Chapter 5

[1] An integrated planning guide for Lent through Eastertide can be found in *Liturgy: From Ashes to Fire,* (A), Vol. 10:2; (B), Vol. 11:2; (C), Vol. 11:4 (Silver Spring: The Liturgical Conference, 1992; 1993; 1994). Also see *Passage to the Paschal Feast, Weeks of Lent,* (A), (B), (C), (Silver Spring: The Liturgical Conference, 1992).

[2] Nathan D. Mitchell, *Eucharist as Sacrament of Initiation,* Forum Essays, No. 2 (Chicago: Liturgy Training Publications, 1994), p. 110.

[3] Mitchell, p. 48.

[4] One reflective guide that can be useful for the newly baptized is Gerard F. Baumbach, *Experiencing Mystagogy: the Sacred Pause of Easter* (New York: Paulist, 1995). The personal reflections in Mark Boyer's *Mystagogy: Liturgical Paschal Spirituality for Lent and Easter* (New York: Alba House, 1990) could be useful for a Holy Saturday retreat, but the thematic arrangement derived from the Easter Vigil ignores the post-Easter lectionary guides.

[5] David Regan, *Experience the Mystery: Pastoral Possibilities for Christian Mystagogy* (Collegeville: The Liturgical Press, 1994), p. 53.

[6] *The Catechumenal Process* (New York: The Church Hymnal Corporation, 1990), especially pp. 74–78. This resource for the Episcopal church provides a variety of pastoral ideas for enhancing the guidance of catechumens and new members.

[7] One resource for the planning of this prayer service is *Liturgy: From Ashes to Fire* (A), Vol. 10:2.

[8] See "The Ministry of the Church," a report of the Joint Lutheran–Roman Catholic Study Commission published in *Origins* 11 (1982): paragraph 85. The context is pp. 295–304.

Selected Bibliography

Anderson, E. Byron. "Performance, Practice and Meaning in Christian Baptism." *Worship* 69:6 (1995): 482–504.

Baumbach, Gerard F. *Experiencing Mystagogy: the Sacred Pause of Easter.* New York: Paulist, 1995.

Bernstein, John A. "Christian Affections and the Catechumenate." *Worship* 52:3 (1978): 194–210.

The Catechumenal Process. New York: The Church Hymnal Corporation, 1990. Resources for the Episcopal Church.

Collins, Mary, OSB. *Worship: Renewal to Practice.* Washington: The Pastoral Press, 1986.

Chupungco, Anscar, OSB. *Worship: Beyond Inculturation.* Washington: The Pastoral Press, 1994.

Dallen, James. "Liturgical Spirituality: Living What We Sing About." *Liturgical Ministry* 4 (1995), 49–59.

Dooley, Catherine. "Liturgical Catechesis: Mystagogy, Marriage or Misnomer." *Worship* 66:5 (1992): 386–397.

Downey, Michael, ed. *That They Might Live: Power, Empowerment and Leadership in the Church.* New York: Crossroad, 1993.

Dunning, James B. *Echoing God's Word: Formation for Catechists and Homilists in a Catechumenal Church.* Arlington: The North American Forum on the Catechumenate, 1993.

Ferrone, Rita. *On the Rite of Election.* Forum Essays, No. 3. Chicago: Liturgy Training Publications, 1994.

Irwin, Kevin. *Liturgy, Prayer and Spirituality.* New York: Paulist, 1984.

Jackson, Pamela. *Journeybread for the Shadowlands: The Readings for the Rites of the Catechumenate, RCIA.* Collegeville: The Liturgical Press, 1993.

Johnson, Maxwell, ed. *Living Water, Sealing Spirit: Readings in Christian Initiation.* Collegeville: The Liturgical Press/Pueblo, 1995.

Joncas, Jan Michael. *Preaching the Rites of Christian Initiation.* Forum Essays, No. 4. Chicago: Liturgy Training Publications, 1994.

Kavanagh, Aidan. *The Shape of Baptism: The Rite of Christian Initiation.* New York: Pueblo, 1978.

Liturgy: From Ashes to Fire, Planning for the Paschal Season, (A), Vol. 10:2; *(B),* Vol. 11:2; *(C),* Vol. 11:4. Silver Spring, MD: The Liturgical Conference, 1992–1994.

Madigan, Shawn, CSJ. *Spirituality Rooted in Liturgy.* Washington: Pastoral Press, 1988.

Mazzo, Enrico. *Mystagogy: A Theology of Liturgy in a Patristic Age,* trans. Matthew J. O'Connell. New York: Pueblo, 1989.

Mitchell, Leonel L. *Worship: Initiation and the Churches.* Washington: The Pastoral Press, 1991.

Mitchell, Nathan D. *Eucharist as Sacrament of Initiation.* Forum Essays, No. 2. Chicago: Liturgy Training Publications, 1994.

Morris, Thomas H. *The RCIA: Transforming the Church.* New York: Paulist, 1989.

_____. *Walking Together in Faith: A Workbook for Sponsors.* New York: Paulist, 1992

Passage to the Paschal Feast, A, B, C. Silver Spring, MD: The Liturgical Conference, 1992.

Power, David N. *The Eucharistic Mystery: Revitalizing the Tradition.* New York: Crossroad, 1992.

Reedy, William J. *Becoming a Catholic Christian.* New York: Sadlier, 1995.

Regan, David. *Experience the Mystery: Pastoral Possibilities for Christian Mystagogy.* Collegeville: The Liturgical Press, 1994.

Rite of Christian Initiation of Adults. Study Edition. Washington: United States Catholic Conference, 1988.

Tufano, Victoria M., ed. *Celebrating the Rites of Adult Initiation: Pastoral Reflections.* Chicago: Liturgy Training Publications, 1992.

Vincie, Catherine. "Gender Analysis and Christian Initiation." *Worship* 69:6 (1995): 505–530.

_____. *The Role of the Assembly in Christian Initiation.* Forum Essays, No. 1. Chicago: Liturgy Training Publications, 1993.

Wilde, James A., ed. *Commentaries: Rite of Christian Initiation of Adults.* Chicago: Liturgy Training Publications, 1988.

_____. *Before and After Baptism.* Chicago: Liturgy Training Publications, 1988.

Zimmerman, Joyce Ann, CPPS. *Liturgy as Living Faith: A Liturgical Spirituality.* Scranton: University of Scranton Press, 1993.